Born with woods and trees for best friends, E.L. Saje became captivated by reading and writing before she turned six. She continued with study in a university faculty among the top 35 in global ranking, and completed an MA in English literature and language. Saje pursued another MA in German literature and language, and she holds a BA level in phonetics. Among her interests are evocative imagination and matters of life beyond façades of human behaviour and religions, as well as social and psychological games people play. A keen lover of English poetry, writing poems has assured Saje throughout joys and those intense, dark sorrows life has brought her way with no prior warning from Lady Luck. By nature, Ellie is a dog lover and a tenacious rebel.

To my wonderful daughter Lisa Katherine, in gratitude for all the love she so generously showers on me.

E.L. Saje

Brian Jones, the Founder of the Rolling Stones

Culprit by Convention

Austin Macauley Publishers

LONDON · CAMBRIDGE · NEW YORK · SHARJAH

Copyright © E.L. Saje 2024

The right of E. L. Saje to be identified as author of this work has been asserted by the author in accordance with sections 77 and 78 of the Copyright, Designs and Patents Act 1988.

All rights reserved. No part of this publication may be reproduced, stored in a retrieval system, or transmitted in any form or by any means, electronic, mechanical, photocopying, recording, or otherwise, without the prior permission of the publishers.

Any person who commits any unauthorised act in relation to this publication may be liable to criminal prosecution and civil claims for damages.

The story, experiences, and words are the author's alone.

A CIP catalogue record for this title is available from the British Library.

Cover photograph by *Gered Mankowitz / Iconic Images*
Brian Jones art illustration by *Erika Fields*

ISBN 9781035842100 (Paperback)
ISBN 9781035842117 (ePub e-book)

www.austinmacauley.com

First Published 2024
Austin Macauley Publishers Ltd®
1 Canada Square
Canary Wharf
London
E14 5AA

My fond gratitude to everyone who has written anything at all about Brian Jones; your books have proved invaluable for my comparative approach in the writing of this book. Many thanks to Laura Jackson, Terry Rawlings, Bill Wyman, Paul Trynka and Nicholas Fitzgerald in particular, and many thanks to newspaper reporters, magazine writers and providers of internet information. Endless thanks to my university teachers and lecturers for their inspiring views and encouragement over my 11 years of university study. You instilled in me the appreciation for literature, writing, art and beauty, which already filled my mind in high school. I am grateful to you for showing me how art, music, song, literature, writing, psychology, philosophy and all matters spiritual and joyous find their way together in all artistic impression, which begins when you feel joy bursting out in your heart, or tears of pain run down your face. The understanding of yourself lets the sun reach into your heart, and the joyous exhilaration opens doors to see incredible beauty, which is the essence of all art.

There is nothing new under the sun, and the joys and sorrows that a modern artist in possession of a creative force experiences are the themes repeated in human history over and over again. They are mythological forces in various manifestations, as experienced by humans; mythological here does not mean a myth with no meaning. It is a description of the same phenomenon shared by millions of people throughout history, and it is ever-present in literature, music and human life. They were strongly present in the life of Brian Jones, too.

My fond thanks to the household darling doggie Nessa for her dogged determination to do whatever she wants in retaliation to commands given, which always inspires me to see another way. Joyous thanks to the brilliant members of our fantastic Facebook group *Brian Jones–The Only Stone*; you are my inspiration. And finally, very special thanks to artist Erika Fields, an indefatigable Brian Jones enthusiast with a gift of excellence to produce fine drawings of Brian Jones in pencil and watercolour.

Table of Contents

Dedication of Direction	13
1. His Flawed Character	15
2. Sweet Cheltenham, Religion and Daddy Dearest	21
3. Did His Parents Love Him?	44
4. I Cannot Breathe!	77
5. Why Brian Would Not Marry	85
6. Just Another Social Bastard?	109
7. Brian the Artist	125
8. Brian Jones and Nicholas Fitzgerald	144
9. Was It a Premature Death?	149
10. The 'Bribed Pathologist' and Other Nasties	176
11. What Was Brian Wearing?	186
12. Hyde Park 5 July 1969	201
Annexures	205
Bibliography	221
References	224

Dedication of Direction

You can't make a silk purse out of a sow's ear, as the saying goes, meaning you cannot turn something inherently inferior into something valuable. The saying dates back to peasants and clergymen in the English and Scottish rural societies of by-gone centuries, although if you asked farm animals, they would strongly disagree about what humans claim is valuable. Apart from such potential differences of opinion in the matter, the old proverb has been proved wrong: Mr Arthur D. Little, an industrialist from Massachusetts, produced a glue from the skin and gristle of pigs' ears in 1921. The glue emerged as fine, colourless streams, which hardened to form a fibre. After that, the fibre was woven into a cloth on a handloom, then cut and made into a purse. So, yes, you can make a fine purse out of a sow's ear, and although silk it did not turn out to be, silk was only a symbol of something beautiful and precious in the original proverb. It seems that the only wisdom we can draw from this is not to take anything for granted, and what we value is not a straight-forward matter.

In order to appreciate the value of something you must first know what you are talking about, and the predecessor of knowledge of something is an understanding of it. You learn the alphabet at rate so that you can then use it to learn more through reading, reasoning and consideration, which skills will enable you to explain and elaborate. The alphabet is only one of the hundreds of basic methods required to open doors, just like chemistry classes at school equip you with an ability to see more, wider and deeper, to discover combinations you never knew existed. You develop an understanding beyond the face value of what seems to be the case, which is always restricted by your own perceptions anyway. Your perception is never a reliable source of factual information.

Understanding grows in solitude and humility. You must welcome the possibility that something you never considered may actually be the truth, or an important aspect you have overlooked. You need to consider and accept that you may have been wrong all along, and you must not guide your perceptions towards a pre-set goal. The overwhelming challenge in learning is that the more you learn, the better you realize how very little you will ever be able to grasp: from a tiny point of knowledge shooting stars explode in every three-dimensional direction of further possibilities and avenues. The thrill and reward is not the result, but the meandering roads you cover on your way towards your goal, and you may be able to enrich the vision of others and deepen their understanding as well.

It may still be that you can't make a silk purse out of a sow's ear, at least in some cases. But before rushing to decide in which context the saying applies, do bear in mind that beauty will always be in the eye of the beholder, and there are no two ways about it. So, please: do re-consider Brian Jones.

1
His Flawed Character

It is a truth universally acknowledged that a person in possession of an intent to write about the Rolling Stones founder Brian Jones must be in want to discuss his flawed character. Because that is the way it must be, and should it occur that Brian avoids being called a devil's disciple in the writer's hands, he cannot escape being at least called a rogue. Other expressions typically used are 'he had a complex character', he was 'a difficult person', he had 'character deficiencies', or 'he was a great musician, but …', and then the negatives begin to pour in. Allegedly he had some of the devil in him, and he was callous, cruel, ruthless, a misogynist and a maniac engaging in 'abnormal' sex. All manner of four-letter words and abusive expressions have been used about him, also by other Rolling Stones members, whom Brian thought were his friends. The unspoken rule is that if you say something positive about him, you must remember to throw in a whole list of negatives to balance it out, as it were, because an objective person would not comment on him in a positive way only. Doing that makes you 'obsessed with him' straight away, whereas mastering up a whole list of negatives about Brian makes you objective and balanced, because he was bad, after all, which had to be proven anyway. It seems like crowds worldwide have been fed a story of a bad, bad Brian Jones by those still in the position of power and probably in possession of a bad conscience about treating Brian in a miserable way; make him out a bad person, and then he deserved what he was dished out by others. The severely flawed argument presented is that mistreating Brian was not the fault of those who did it, because they would not have done it, had Brian not been so bad. But the dead cannot argue back.

When Brian Jones founded his group the Rolling Stones in 1962, it was still the post-war era of the old and firmly established gender roles in England. Such old traditions needed more than polishing off the corners, and were it not for the war effort and the surge of hope in all areas of life, it is likely the decade would not have turned out the major decade of social upheaval. But the 1960s emerged like a radiant spring season, and the decade changed traditions in a multitude of ways, challenged by young English men and women pursuing education, wealth, opportunity, careers and personal freedom like never before in the English history. For the first time ever, women were allowed to express their sexuality, and their keenness to do so quickly grew out of all constraints, like a yeast dough left in a sunny spot.

In the 1960s, married women were called women or ladies, but there was no real expression for young women between their teens and the time they got married. A concept of a woman in her own right did not exist, and women were defined by way of their connection to a man. Little girls became bigger girls until they married or reached menopause, at which point in time they became obsolete; between the start of menstruation and the end thereof, they were either married women and ladies, or shop girls, sales girls, office girls, career girls, good girls, bad girls, bunny girls and call girls.

Brian's Rolling Stones were young guys with lots of energy and a testosterone level to match, so they went for it, as did the 'girls'. The Stones always talked about girls and not women, and they probably thought nothing further about it. Not because they were misogynists and wanted to run down females, but because they were part of an era marked with a change from established conformity to something new. That something new would be society changing further in the direction of feminist movements, but that time had not come yet. Attitudes and social perceptions do not change in a couple of years, and this is reflected in the Stones oscillating between calling women 'girls' or just 'women'.

Then there are all those rumours and allegations about Brian's 'abnormal' sex life; how would anyone not involved know? Perhaps those making such comments are not getting enough sex themselves, or are not getting the kind of sex they really would like, so jealousy and envy in small minds decide there must be something wrong with Brian who did just that. Everybody likes sex in one form or another. Sex feels good. It feels very good. In fact, it feels so good that there must be something wrong with it. Especially if it happens in circumstances outside your own life circles. In any society, life circles of the majority, or those in a position of power, are always deemed the standard 'normal', despite such 'normal' sex sounding like a boring routine.

All there is available are unfounded allegations not made by Brian or women Brian knew, and no complaints were made by women who were involved, yet rotten comments by third parties have been made about Brian in the context. Common sense should say it is not possible to say what happens in other people's intimate privacy, and Brian Jones had his privacy just as much as anyone else has theirs. But if you are sexually active in a heterosexual relationship and do it missionary on Wednesday and Saturday, there is no doubt that the flesh has gone cold and the mind has seized up. Any adult not engaging in S&M, or something else they fancy, be it feathers, a whole chicken, dress-ups or things X-rated, should not think they are better than others or 'more normal' in any which way. They may well be just too inhibited and lacking in imagination. A bit of spanking or other things spicy and stingy might add a sweet cherry on top of other ways pleasurable that cause a happy laughter in the middle of the night; the one you keep hearing from your next-door neighbour's bedroom. An awful neighbour on their side or sour grapes on yours?

The claims and scenarios about Brian's 'flawed character' have not offered any explanation why his 'flawed character' was the case, if it ever was, or why it would have been. It just seems as if Mother Nature went and randomly whacked a weird head on his shoulders and everything flowed from there. Yet it obviously did not happen like that; it does not happen like that with anyone. We are all born and grow into adults, and while genetics play their role, we all have a childhood history, and our experiences directly affect who we are and how we act in our relationships. It was no different for Brian Jones, and the whys and wherefores are what this book wants to discuss, to perhaps broaden the horizons of those who like him or dislike him alike. And perhaps give an understanding and a new angle to many issues and situations which Brian has been blamed for in the most minute of detail.

The interest in Brian Jones continues as strong as ever, and the extent to which Brian's conduct in his relationships has been scrutinized over the past decades would easily convince the most reasonable observer that Brian was the only party responsible for what unfolded ever. Indeed, Brian has been placed under the lens of a microscope and dissected like a moth, and the staunchest advocate of objective thinking would be persuaded that he was nothing but a flawed troublemaker who exclusively ruined his affairs. This goes in particular for his relationships with women, but also his adult relationships with men, and fault invariably falls on Brian only. The only exception where no blame is laid on Brian is his relationship with his parents, although, by the same token, in this instance no blame is laid on anyone, and no comment is made on who was responsible and for what. On grounds unknown, his parents fall in a category best titled 'do not touch', especially in social media. Other than that, it is as if Brian was the only person who contributed to what happened before or after a relationship, and an aftermath there always was, because none of his relationships were lasting ones. He passed away at a young age, but in those seven or eight adult years of his many bridges were burnt, and goodbyes were bitter and laden with tears.

Every writer or critic, when immersing himself in the shredding of Brian's private life into miniscule segments of blame on his part, has had the benefit of hindsight. Add to that the luxury that no matter how hard they have disparaged Brian, he has not been there to make a comment or defend himself. Obviously, it is more convenient to blame the dead and not make waves, so as not to step on the toes of those who wish to cling onto their shiny self-image, fabricated or otherwise, and would not welcome blame. And so it has become to pass that there was no relationship whose break-up was deemed the fault of someone other than Brian. Admittedly, Brian was always party to his private relationships; it takes two to tango, as they say. Except with Brian he became the culprit of all things evil and the other party an innocent victim who did nothing remotely unfair or unjust.

That it 'takes two to tango' does not mean the fault for problems or failures that arise should be shared equally. In fact, it does not mean that the fault should be shared in any proportion. It only means that a relationship, encounter or event between two people has two parties. To think otherwise is a total blunder; while it does take two, the other one may be completely innocent apart from being present at whatever happened. Think of an assault: yes, it does take two to tango, but only the villain can be held responsible for what happened, because the victim was merely present, or, indeed, was very much trying not to be present but could not get away. Yet it is very much the case that it took 'two to tango' for the assault to occur, because there had to be two people to make the assault possible. And that is all the saying means: two are involved, but, as such, there is no allocation of fault or guilt in any proportion. However, people typically twist it in their minds to mean equal fault, except with Brian Jones the saying has been twisted further to make him the only bad party. And a very bad party indeed.

2
Sweet Cheltenham, Religion and Daddy Dearest

Brian's parents lived in southern Wales before migrating to Cheltenham at an unknown time before Brian's birth in early 1942. It was still the time of World War 2, and Wales did not escape bombing. In fact, it was heavily bombed during the war, and Cardiff Blitz, as the German Luftwaffe attacks were called in the area between 1940 and 1944, caused great damage and unease in the relatively small area. It may be that the civilian loss of ca. 355 can be said to be small, but it was 355 too many, and concern for safety was paramount. In 1940 and 1941 Cardiff and the surrounding areas, as well as western Wales, were heavily targeted by the Luftwaffe. The uncertainty of the times and the heavy bombings are likely to have been the incentive for the family of Mr Lewis Jones and his wife Mrs Jones to look for a safer place for their family-to-be, and Cheltenham was not only a safe area but also reasonably close, relatively speaking. How close it was exactly and how awkward it was to migrate is hard to assess, because infrastructures were completely different and any damage caused during the war was repaired and rebuilt only after the war. Suffice to say beautiful Bristol Bridge was there, having been built in 1768, but M4 and M5 did not exist until 1962.

But Cheltenham was much safer than Wales at the time, and it was safer than large cities Birmingham and London. Indeed, children from those cities were sent to greener and quieter Cheltenham for safety from the war. While Cheltenham did not escape unharmed, the damage of Cheltenham bombing in July 1942 was minor, and little Brian, 6 months old at the time, as well as his parents, had a Cheltenham home safe from external damage. Soon after the end of the war, the town was busy with rebuilding, and there was no shortage of employment, with business investments increasing in the area, which further attracted skilled professionals like Brian's father. The small town was like an open invitation that guaranteed employment in the comfort of peaceful, green fields and bird song.

Cheltenham in the 1940s and 1950s was a town of ca. 60,000 people huddled comfortably in the safe embrace of the hills on the east and the areas gently sloping down to the sea to the west. It was a lovely place with lovely houses, lovely hillocks, lovely lawns and lovely families with lovely parents and children. It was the lovely town in which Brian's parents wanted to continue their life. Their wishes and dreams were very conservative and they looked the affluent part: a well-dressed, educated father employed by a big company and a smiling, musical mother in charge of domestic bliss cooked in her kitchen of Wedgewood porcelain and shiny pots and pans, all picture perfect as were her permed hair and a pearl necklace. Life was smooth and pleasant, and regular Church attendance on Sunday the norm.

It must have been storks that brought Cheltenham babies in cloth bundles and left them at the married parents' doorsteps, unless an undutiful stork cut corners to land on the roof top and dropped the baby through the chimney. It must have been, because sex was a three-letter word not mentioned, and it was up to the youngsters to learn about flowers and bees. The parental intent behind this was to leave children to learn about such things as late as possible, and, of course, children would take it upon themselves to learn about such matters the sooner the better; the charm of the forbidden always makes it all the more interesting and desirable regardless of age. The fake, rosy, religious façade only ever allowed married men and women to engage in physical relations. Those relations meant conservative love making, which had to become a more and more spiritual experience distanced from the physical bodies that made it happen; perish the thought of hot sex or sex talk to excite. Mortification of the flesh was the objective, and doggie style sex was a carnal evil best nipped on the bud, unless the Head of the Family was inclined to Christian domestic discipline and thereby required to spank the backside of his wife. A requirement it was then, as it was his duty, of course, to correct and punish her for her errors, and only a wicked person with dark motives would suggest that the Head of the Family enjoyed the regular duty he religiously chose to adhere to; duty binds and a loving heart is devoted. A good wife would dutifully succumb to her husband's wishes in the bedroom, which she did not enjoy any more than wine; a good, religious wife would only drink wine for thirst. Despite the high number of children born out of wedlock in the lovely town of Cheltenham, extra-marital affairs were a taboo not mentioned, and wives, neatly cutting their Chelsea buns in quarters and smiling demurely over cups of tea, would not talk about their husbands' unexplained absences from their domestic bliss. Mothers of those golden families were busy planning a married life for their daughters before they could fall pregnant.

And into this hypocritical world of appearances, perfectionism, warped ideas and lack of basic understanding of psychology, a sweet, innocent baby boy called Brian Jones was born on 28 February 1942. He was the first-born in the Jones family of paternal Christian family hierarchy of authoritarian values and principles. He was the only son of the family with 3 children, one of whom tragically died of leukaemia very early on. Brian was to be the one to carry the family name onto future generations, as his sister would change her family name on marriage. So, the plan was for Brian to become like his father and excel in education to land a job only the cream of young hopefuls would qualify for. A respectable job it was to be, one that would throw doors wide open to an outstanding career, and as a sideline he would marry a lovely Christian virgin to produce Jones babies in the third Cheltenham generation. It was what the parents wanted for their lives, and the thought that it might not be what their children wanted for their own lives probably never occurred to them. The Jones children were going to be marionettes playing the parts their parents had in mind, to keep up the image of a lovely family in lovely Cheltenham of lovely, shady trees and lawns.

Which is pretty much as far as the plan ever got, because school problems arouse for Brian before he became a teen, culminating in suspensions from school, which was a horrifying embarrassment to bear for his mortified parents. By the time Brian turned thirteen in 1955, the dysfunctional family dynamics fell apart abysmally. It was a family catharsis of extraordinary proportions, as tragic as a purifying catharsis in a Greek tragedy, with the exception that the Cheltenham catharsis continued for some ten years, whereas in a Greek tragedy it would typically not last more than a couple of hours. But in Cheltenham pressure had been building up for years, and it could not be suppressed. You cannot suppress pressure ever: pressure will always out.

Brian's father Lewis had been putting a lot of pressure on his young son to make him conform to the paternal wishes, and Brian would not bar of it. Lewis Jones spoke about his son on BBC Radio 4 A Story of our Time in 1971:

"Up to a certain point, Brian was a perfectly normal, conventional little boy, who was well-behaved and well-liked. Well-liked, I suppose, because he was well-behaved. He did his studies and he was quite a model school-boy. Then there came this peculiar change in his early teens. At the time, I suppose, he began to become a man, where he began to get some resentment of authority. It was a rebellion against parental authority, and it was certainly a rebellion against a school authority. He often used to say, why should he do something he was told, just because the person who was telling him was older."

It is self-evident that Brian's argument was right, but it is equally self-evident that his father disagreed; instead of priding in his son's logical and smart thinking, his words echo disappointment and disapproval. Lewis Jones also found that the school had not gone the right way about disciplining young Brian, and in that regard he very much sounds like a modern parent; one of those who think their little blossom can do no wrong, and the responsibility of bringing up their little darling lies with the school. Why do they not think they are responsible for bringing up their own children? Alas, they are every modern teacher's nightmare, because teachers would be more than happy to teach children the three Rs reading, writing and arithmetic as well as provide high school education to teens, if only they did not have to deal with immature parents and bring them up as well as a sideline. So, Brian's father was very much ahead of his time, and as such a regular visitor to see Dr Bell, the headmaster of Cheltenham Grammar School. They did not have a particularly warm relationship, because of the on-going complaints beyond educational issues that Brian's father kept making to Dr Bell. A good example is Brian's father demanding that Dr Bell arrange for a haircut for young Brian.

Brian's form teacher Mr Jim Dodge wrote in Brian's school report for September 1954 to July 1955 that Brian "suffered from a dominating father & had to show off to compensate." The report was sent home with Brian, and it is not known how Dear Father reacted on reading it. But undoubtedly he and Dear Mother both had feelings about it.

Dear Father's approach to parenting was one in which parents decide about everything for their children and children do as they are told, because their parents are older, and because that is just the way things are. No point in challenging a given. Dear Father perhaps anticipated some occasional discontent and grumbling, but he was confident that his chosen direction was going to remain undisputed. Considering himself superior to his son by rank, he did not hesitate to make ultimatums such as 'you shall do as I say, or else'! Now the tricky thing with ultimatums always is that you may end up shooting yourself in the foot, so do consider your own position carefully, before raising your voice with an ultimatum. However, this line of thinking was alien to any alternatives Father Dearest could fathom, so Brian could like it or lump it, but nothing would change.

But what Father Dearest did not anticipate was that Brian chose to lump it and dump it. A pink elephant landing in the backyard was a more likely option. But happen it did, and Daddy and Mommy Dearest had to deal with something they did not know existed. The more pressure they put on Brian, the harder Brian resisted and kept to his own direction. Which was the only reasonable way forward for him, because he had his own life ahead and he had to live it in his way. He had to do his own thing, and Father and Mother Dearest forgot that children only listen, when they feel listened to, and that the way parents talk to their children becomes the children's inner voice.

Brian's parents wanted to control Brian, because he was not voluntarily doing what they wanted him to do, and they no less than bullied him in their attempts to make him comply. They failed totally, entirely and completely, with Brian rebelling against them with all his might. Brian's rebellion was unwanted and appalling from his parents' point of view, but the falling out of Brian and his parents was a secondary matter. The major tragedy were the consequences of the parents' bullying efforts on Brian. He rebelled to get free, and every time his parents tried to enforce authoritative rules to control him, he rebelled by doing the opposite.

Like all other children, Brian was a child in the hands of his parents, and the power imbalance was not in his favour. But every time he rebelled, the power imbalance remained unchanged, and he was just as much under his parents' control as before. Brian did not rebel out of his free choice; his rebellion was an automatic reaction, no different from you pulling your hand back, if you burn your finger. Not that he or his parents were aware of it, and so his parents continued to control him just as much as they had before he rebelled. Brian's acts of rebellion were jack-in-the-box reactions: every time you open the lid, the figure on the spring inside the box pops out. Equally, every time Brian's parents tried to enforce rules unacceptable to Brian, he reacted with a rebellious act against the very thing or rule the parents tried to force on him.

Had he rebelled out of free choice, he would have helped his personal growth in an excellent way, but he was too young to understand better. When you form an opinion of a matter that is unacceptable to you, you rebel, and perhaps decide to do something about it with a goal ahead. But it then does not throw your whole life into chaos, because you have other sides to your personality, and perhaps a mental balance of some sort. Brian was too young and inexperienced to know what mental balance was, and he probably never saw it displayed at home. He did not have an opportunity to develop a balanced personality in his childhood, because he had to fight parental oppression, and it was too late to do in adulthood, because it needed to be done in childhood, in order for a reasonably balanced adult to develop.

Naturally, his mind was in constant chaos, because he was young and vulnerable under the oppressive control of his parents, whose only goal was to make him what they wanted him to be. So he did what he felt was all he could do, and systematically went against everything his parents stood for, and that meant any rules of society and its religions. He rebelled against the power of his father and the society his father represented, and chose actions that went against the values of the two. Of course, none of this went down well with Daddy Dearest in particular, and because Brian's father and Cheltenham society were in a position of power over Brian, his rebellion usually had a bad outcome. Rebellion was the method he used to try and gain balance. His rebellion in every field of life was the first step he had to take to become free, but he needed to go further, far further, to learn how to live. He never got there, and rebellion became for him an exercise seeking to justify the end; to Brian, his need to rebel was the explanation and justification of his actions. All along, Brian had the initial, automatic spark to start a fire, but not the understanding to use his fuel in a constructive way. Regrettably, Brian's actions went totally against his father's conviction of patriarchalism deeply rooted in the Christian tradition and anything that he and his household in Cheltenham firmly stood for.

Western culture and Christian religion distinctly uphold the supremacy of parental authority in general and paternal infallibility in particular. It is not that there should be degrees or areas of compromise, but the authority is absolute without variation. Most of us have grown up in this system so much so that we do not even notice the rules instilled in us are contradictory, let alone do we question their validity. We are typically taught 'do not talk back to your mother' or 'do not shout at your father', whereas shouting at siblings or other people is not a violation of such enormity. Yes, it does amount to bad manners or sibling rivalry, but shouting at one's parents is tantamount to sacrilege. Equally, any later criticism of one's parents is shushed away with 'they did their best' or 'they were only trying to help', and should you dare to raise your contradictory voice, you are silenced off with a contemptuous and self-righteous command 'do not judge'. Control continues from the grave, because any complaint made is typically dismissed with 'do not talk ill of the dead'. How can a confused, young child go to his or her mother and tell her that 'Daddy keeps touching me *there* and it hurts'? When will a child ever be able to have a discussion of mistakes his parents make, when unwelcome comments are denied and differences of opinion are seen as personal attacks against the omnipotent father who is always right, and if he is not right, at least the child is wrong, and the right solution is elsewhere for the father to resource? When will there be a time for a child, or an adult child, to say to the parents that it may be they did their best, but it was not enough, or it was not what was needed?

Brian's parents were ambitious, churchy people whose past is rather unknown, apart from them coming from Wales, where they also returned sometime after Brian's passing in 1969. But they were devoted Christians, be it good or bad, and their values were patriarchal perceptions of how they understood the New Testament. So, when they arrived in Cheltenham, they probably envisaged a future in the safe hands of the Almighty, as they understood was the case, and their Christian perception of the Great Yonder was a domicile under the care and authority of the Loving God who protected and provided. Their lives were controlled by their beliefs and religious doctrines and practices, and their home a miniature establishment of the same patriarchal system, with the father figure as omnipotent and wise as the Loving God who continued and continued to provide and protect, even if it did not always feel that way.

Brian's father Lewis Blount Jones was born in 1917, and his mother Louisa Beatrice Simmonds in 1918, so when their son Brian was born in 1942, they were 24–25 years old. It would appear that his mother's first name used to be Pansy and she changed it, but whether or not, they came from Wales, and the locality had a church and some necessities even a small township needed, but there was no grand future there for anyone. It is reasonable to think their upbringing was conservative and the paternal and religious influences were intense and strict, considering it was the early 1900s in a small, remote and religious Welsh corner of the world. Cheltenham must have seemed a wonderful opportunity for a bright and prosperous future, and, as always, their Loving God would guide, provide and protect. But Cheltenham was not the small place like the small township in Wales, and social structures were different, with the added complication that English society was going to change fast after the war.

Christian patriarchalism comes with its problems, one of the predominant ones being that while the Loving God protects and provides, it happens from somewhere outside our world. That means that people carry on about their daily business detached from things religious, and then approach religious issues separately at an appropriate time, much in the way one puts an apron on for cooking or gardening gloves for pulling out weeds, but not otherwise. The method to approach and talk to Him is to pray, and when you do, He will listen and respond. He has the control of all situations, but He listens and provides what you need, which you assume will be what you want, although what we want and what we need tend to be lightyears apart. And when it turns out you did not get what you prayed for, you stomp your foot, kick up a fuss and feel sorry for yourself allegedly let down. Yet any mature and reasonable way of thinking would understand that the God-Force, regardless of what it may mean to different individuals, is not a life insurance to safeguard you from problems you do not want to deal with. And that is because life is not the pleasant illusion left when all problems have been removed.

Quite the opposite: all those problems are part of your life, and you must deal with them as best you can. After all, the God-Force gave people a brain for thinking and problem solving, as one would easily assume, and it seems to work for the purpose. People think we were given hands so we can work; people think we were given legs and feet so we can walk; people think we were given eyes so we can see. But why do people think we were given our brain to let it run at idle, instead of using it for problem solving and running our lives?

That, of course, would mean that you take responsibility for your life and choices, which can turn out inconvenient. It is much easier to place the responsibility somewhere else, known or unknown, and play the victim, when things go wrong. It is easy to convince yourself that there is a Force that protects you from life, and the method to approach the Force is to pray. So, pray you must and answer He will.

However, in this scenario He is no different from Santa: write a letter and Santa will deliver, but if you have been naughty, you will not get what you wanted. As profoundly stupid as it sounds, people really think in this way. Except if you ask them whether they really do think in this way, they will laugh off the question with an almost convincing 'Of course I don't'! And then they continue exactly as before without realizing that the naïve belief system they still hold on to has turned into a ridiculous 'request and it shall be delivered' fairy-tale.

And as luck would have it, fairy-tales run their course and life does not have a guarantee for a happy ending. It also happened in the family of Lewis and Louisa Jones, after they had arrived in the Cheltenham, their new land of milk and honey. It happened after Brian was less than two years old, when their first daughter, Pamela, born in October 1943, developed leukaemia and passed away less than two weeks after her second birthday in October 1945. It must have been a horrendous blow to the parents, and traditional Christians typically think of such things as a punishment to the parents, which, of course, they are not. At times like this, people doubt their belief systems and questions are asked: why did the Loving God not prevent it? Such questions may receive an answer, but only in private moments of those directly affected.

However, and as blinkered religious minds will be aware, there is always the highway to immediate feelings of happiness and righteousness in prayer or intense reading of the Bible. Reading the Bible is already a good thing *per se*, whether you understand what you are reading or not. But if you do not, perhaps you just need to read more intensely, because these things work in mysterious ways? Attending a religious service will do the same trick; as if by magic, it encases you in the comforting cape of being good and virtuous, which will soon distract you from those feelings of sadness and misery. Not to mention anger, which you must not feel, but if you still do, as you invariably will, you can hide it in more intense prayer to push the anger further down still, thereby lighting the fire under the pressure cooker of your mind. And away the brew will, until the lid blows off and you can no longer run away from what you really hold inside.

Along came another daughter in August 1946, and Brian's mommy dearest doted on the new, younger sister henceforth. From then on, until Brian's problems at school became an issue some six or seven years later, the family probably experienced its happiest times, children and parents included. The wound from the lost daughter Pamela must have remained with the parents and distressed them, and life must have seemed more fragile than it did before her passing. The joy over the second daughter was overwhelming, and the rest of the family may not have taken much notice of Brian going through his formative years and absorbing like a sponge the spoken and unspoken rules of the family life. But things were still manageable and under control for the parents. After all, they had Brian and their second daughter Barbara, and Brian would carry on the family name. So, all in all, things were pretty honky-dory.

Then Brian, innocently and with no ill intent like everyone else, went and turned ten, and his hormones started waking up. It was the beginning of a new phase of life for Lewis and Louisa Jones, and they had not planned for this one. With Brian turning alternative and free range with no familiar label to attach on, the parents felt they were losing control of their son Brian. Well, they were, and they ultimately did, but far more than that, they lost control of their domestic world they insisted must be as they decided. They wanted their life with frames firm and safe, appearances neat and pleasant, and values pre-set and solid. Yet in reality, their world was in the middle of an earth quake zone they brought with them. Their world was but a couple of reeds erected on shaky grounds, and the wind blew them away and scattered the pieces in all four directions, for them to rebuild themselves a world new and better. And their failure was that they did not do it. Because had they done so, Brian would have been saved, too.

Despite the Jones family of absolute patriarchal authority trembling and collapsing, Brian's parents did not change their ways. In the face of adversity with the first daughter's passing and Brian not conforming to paternal wishes, Lewis Jones was undoubtedly asking himself why his Loving God was not protecting and providing. Alas, Lewis Jones was blind to any other way, and if the response he received was for him to adjust his ways, he did not understand it. What other way? It may well be he had never thought of another way, so his way was always right and anything else was wrong, and when things are wrong, they are evil, because only evil brings wrong with it. While the logic of that is undeniable, its corroding weakness is that individual concepts of evil are perceptions only and not fact, and laws of logic do not apply to perceptions of meaning. However, in the Lewis Jones family logic of wrong and right, there was no middle way or grey area of any degree. Just a strict division into black and white, the border between them as absolute as the power that mine fields and barbed wire yielded to keep Western and Eastern Europe apart during the Cold War. Or perhaps he thought it was a test from Somewhere Religious; tradition has trials and tribulations sent to good religious servants to test their devotion and sincerity.

Impossible as it is say what Brian's father and mother were really thinking, one thing is for sure: they were scared. They were very scared and fearful about what was happening to their lives, how things would unfold, and what the future would entail. They had already experienced fear and concern with the war, and had migrated to a safer area. It had been a life change they had chosen at a time they were prepared for, and they had the means and ability go through this life change; it was under control for them. But then, and quite unexpectedly, Brian unwillingly introduced an enormous change and challenge to his parents, which set in motion a topsy-turvy they had no control over. They felt disempowered and bitter. Like all other human beings, they were mere mortals with fears and worries, and the greater the change and challenge, the stronger the hesitation and resistance, because there is no change of direction without risks taken. Would they be willing to risk the safety there used to be? And then there was the congregation, and what on earth would people say?

You will not find a person who will admit that he is a bad driver and an intolerant person. While there are millions of bad drivers and millions of intolerant people, it is incredibly rare to find someone admitting one or the other. While there are further millions who are both bad drivers and intolerant people, would you ever find one admitting to the combination? Our societies require good driving skills, and a guy needs to be able to smoothly operate his vehicle to look cool, and when he grows older, he becomes an experienced driver behind the wheel of his Merc. Women are not any different, unless, if and when they have a car crash, they throw themselves into the pattern of a helpless damsel in distress; looking and sounding helpless may remove the responsibility from the driver. Until that should occur, they are confident and capable drivers behind the wheel of their Ford.

Intolerance is an absolute socially forbidden, and it goes against the basic ideas and values of a multicultural society where good citizens listen, appreciate and understand values and principles different from their own. It is the social expectation, whether it stems from Christian values or elsewhere, and if it stems from Christian values, it is non-negotiable and sinful to do otherwise. Again, patriarchalism brings its own complications; a father looking and sounding intolerant cannot be, because he is infallible, so the child must be wrong. But if a Christian man should appear intolerant to a peer of his, the issue would rise that one or the other must step down from their Christian patriarchal pedestal; one must be wrong, but how can that be, because they are both infallible?

This was one of the problems Brian's parents were having, because if they were to change their absolute patriarchal values, it was very likely that a gap would open between them and others in their equally unstable boats of patriarchalism, and who would be the first to admit their boat was taking on water and might even sink? That all boats of Cheltenham church attendees were beautifully afloat and nobody had grounds for concern was one of those unspoken rules never mentioned. In any case, things had to be right by the end of the week for the Sunday morning service, where loving religious ears struggled weekly at the mercy of the church choir of older men and women singing with a fond enthusiasm their thin voices out of tune could not possibly justify. But if you asked anyone after the service, they would attest with a smile that it had been uplifting, like it always was.

It is easy to understand that Brian's parents would have had to make enormous sacrifices to their values and routines, if the family system were to change to benefit Brian, so that there need not be the constant fighting regarding family hierarchy. Against that background, nothing could change, and nothing did. The justification of their choices lies in their conviction of the patriarchal home life being the one and only way. They were self-absorbed and totally self-centred in their relationship with Brian, which raises the question, where they bad parents?

First and foremost, they were mere mortals, and they made mistakes like everybody else does. It is absolutely fine to shout at your children at times, when you lose your calm, as long as it does not become your standard way of conversation with your children. Parents have problems of their own, and they can feel tired and exhausted, which is typically the background for an anger burst from a parent; it explains, although it does not excuse. Brian's parents would not have been any different, and there was no need for them to be perfect ever. What is essential is how often it happened, how intense it was, and what happened between the outburst of frustration or anger from the parents. Because if there was nothing but the outbursts and no love expressed verbally and in actions, life was dysfunctional in the household.

A good example of the abysmal state of affairs in the Jones dysfunctional household in early 1961 is a scene of Brian and a girlfriend of his going to see Brian's parents to tell them about their baby on the way. Brian's mother lost her calm completely and verbally abused both Brian and the girlfriend, calling him a bastard and not sparing harsh words on her either. After that Mother Dearest, in her act of uncontrolled rage, ran to Brian's bedroom to grab his guitar and break it to pieces. Then Father Dearest entered the house, and the parental abuse escalated from very bad to worse still, after which the young lovers ran out with Brian's parents still screaming.[1]

The scene described was one of physical and verbal abuse, which commonly occurs in dysfunctional families, and it originates with the parents' conduct. The childhoods and younger years of Brian's parents were in all probability spent in homes just as dysfunctional as the home they were making for their own children. Dysfunctional parents come from dysfunctional homes, repeating the vicious circle of carrying on with destructive ways, which results in more dysfunctional families. Families are not only a group of related people, but a group of people forming a mesh network with multiple interconnections, some of them known to the family members, but most by far unknown forever. This mesh network contains all human emotions, and in this interconnected mesh members of all families experience their life events that involve strong human feelings such as love, hate, anger, dislike, pride and jealousy. Except in dysfunctional families the interconnected mesh turns into an entangled mess, when the smooth surface admitted and permitted is scratched with a sea breeze of something undesired by the parents, presumed to be the responsible authorities in charge. Under the smooth surface that dysfunctional families present to the public hide volcanoes and ravines no less eruptive or deep and treacherous than those under the surface of oceans. Do not judge an ocean by the dolphins playing on the surface.

Every system must have some rules, and every family has rules. In a healthy family they promote individual freedom, growth and contentment. But dysfunctional family life is full of unspoken rules to everybody's detriment. You cannot see them, smell them or touch them, but you can sense them, because they are there. One such significant unspoken rule in Brian's Cheltenham family was that father is always right. It was a game based on unspoken rules:

Unspoken rule 1 Father is always right.
Unspoken rule 2 There is no rule father is always right.
Unspoken rule 3 Everybody knows there is the rule but will pretend not to know.

All young Brian needed to do was to defy what his father told him, and emotional pressure began to build up between the paternal ears, and possibly maternal ears as well; she was part of the same game. Perhaps Brian would ask why his father should be right only because he was older, thereby transgressing the unspoken rules all in one go. And the result would be his mother screaming at him for being disrespectful and his father calling him a bad child. How hurt he would be, how lonely and how empty emotionally, with no right to have feelings! In a dysfunctional family rights are not evenly distributed and privileges belong to the authoritarian parents. Children's needs are not recognized beyond what parents are comfortable with, and children learn this is the right way. Children always trust their parents blindly. If children of controlling parents do what they parents want them to do, they receive love and cuddles. If they do not, love is withdrawn and further controlling enforced, to bring the children back in line and regain the power of control. Sadly, children do conform, because they need the love and cuddles, but underneath uncertainty builds up in their minds and they feel confused. Yet conforming is better than feeling the guilt of not being loyal to your parent, which is a nasty guilt trap for a child.

In a Jones family photograph taken on 1 June 1964, there are three family members sitting on the sofa in the family home. The people are the parents and Brian's younger sister Barbara, born on 22 August 1946, so she was turning 18 in less than three months and was a young woman already. Dressed in clothes that a 10-year-old at the time was likely to wear, although it is always impossible to vouch for personal preferences, she sits there expressionless, looking at neither of her parents or the camera. Her hands are clenched together in her lap, and a small, stuffed, brown teddy, probably no more than four inches high, is sitting on her knee. Her father is sitting on her left and mother on his left. Together, they are holding more small stuffed toys and offering them to their daughter. Her mother is holding a small, stuffed giraffe.

The photo speaks more than the proverbial thousand words would, and you feel totally bewildered looking at it; it does not seem at all possible that a balanced and contented young lady fast approaching her 18th birthday would have any interest in playing with soft toys. It may be the parents needed to keep her as a young child for their own emotional needs, but she definitely needed to get out of there and have an opportunity to grow up.

Did Brian's parents not know how to treat others? Did they not know Matthew 22:37–39 *'Thou shalt love thy neighbour as thyself'*? Well, of course they did, and they understood that 'neighbour' meant any other person. But Brian was not 'another person'. He was his controlling parents' child, and as such an attachment to who the parents were. He was the one to carry on the family name in the very image of his father. In a family with such dominating parents as those Brian had the whole family is dysfunctional. As always, a family system is based on the relationship between the mother and father, and in Brian's family his parents were both dysfunctional themselves, and both married another dysfunctional person to try and complete their individual dysfunctional needs. It was not because they were bad people, but because they themselves came from dysfunctional families. In contrast, balanced and emotionally healthy adults are not needy, and they search for another balanced person for a relationship; they already function as individuals. They have an identity with clear identity borders. They know who they are and what they stand for. In a dysfunctional family all identity borders get enmeshed and become obscured, and the parents lack an insight into their own personalities.

But assuming Brian's parents did know themselves to some extent, which seems very unlikely, he was still a mere addition to his parents. They wanted him to become like themselves. They encouraged his behaviour in that direction, but scolded him, if he tried something he wanted. The family tradition and what the parents wanted for their own future blurred their personal boundaries and those of Brian, and differences of opinion had to amalgamate. Identities gradually dissolved into a family atmosphere, undoubtedly charged and heavy, and you could slice it thick or thin, as long as you knew not the mention there was an atmosphere in the house; one of those unspoken rules nobody mentioned but everybody knew. And when little Brian could not express his wishes without his parents getting upset, he learnt to be quiet for domestic peace. In doing so he was looking after his parents' feelings while denying his own, until he decided to call it off and let the storm clouds ride on from the horizon, where they had been gathering and rumbling for a long time.

3
Did His Parents Love Him?

Brian grew up in a home where he was not allowed to do what he wanted and feel like he did, because his parents decided what he would do, and having feelings was strictly limited in general. His personality did not have an opportunity to develop, and he was downright verbally abused for things that were precious to him. His self-esteem not only suffered but was effectively decimated, and he remained insecure and lacking in self-confidence throughout his life. He did not receive emotional support, and it seems his parents were not capable of showing feelings, apart from anger and disapproval. Warm encouragement and approval were missing. Linda Lawrence, an important girlfriend in Brian's life, describes their visit to his parents on 26 September 1963 as a cold and rigid occasion with Brian's presence in the house essentially ignored, as if he were not there.

It seems Brian's father was better at expressing feelings than his mother, and we do not know if and how his parents expressed love or fondness in their privacy. Lewis Jones still had the burden of the patriarchal tradition in the 1960s society to keep him less expressive than one would be now. But he made his choice for his own comfort and social safety, instead of encouraging his son to go further. There is no need to feel sympathy for Lewis Jones for such a decision; it was the choice he made. The social pressures of Cheltenham communities, whether Christian or not, perhaps help one to understand why he made the choices he did, but none of it was easy on Brian either, and Brian was the more vulnerable one. An explanation of why you do something is not an excuse for doing it, when it is a choice knowingly and voluntarily made. Lewis Jones had the responsibility not only for himself but also for his young son Brian.

Brian's parents did not have empathy or respect for him, so he consequently learnt that he was deserving of that kind of behaviour; a child's trust in the parent is blind and absolute. Later, in the mid-1960s, he did not fight back against other Rolling Stones members, when they apparently pushed him aside from leadership and song writing. He did not understand the irreplaceable value he had to the Rolling Stones music and image. It was easy for others to use him for their purposes, because he felt he did not deserve better. He did not rebel because the other Stones were not authorities in power like his parents were; they were his peers and he thought they were his friends. He never rebelled against his peers in Cheltenham, but withdrew from them instead and became lonely. He accepted that he was treated in an abusive and ugly manner, because it was the way he had always been treated, and he never received respect and kindness in his formative years or in his teens.

When Brian embarked on his journey of what he wanted to do, a major problem for him was the one we all have: our conscious view of what life ought to be seldom corresponds to what life really is. But unlike most, Brian was and remained his genuine self, instead of inhabiting behind the whitewashed facade most by far develop to hide the very nature of their organic being underneath, which is lecherous, foul-smelling and self-protective. You peel all the skin off the onion, and that is what you find inside. Brian refused the moral image of his father to beset him, yet his father's emotional distance from Brian meant their mutual relationship could not develop, which prevented Brian from breaking free. He became torn between the two, and could not move onto the next step of his emotional development.

Statistically, children of dysfunctional families develop substance abuse, which typically relieves the pain from the anxiety they experience, being at a loss with their lives. In an interview published in *Melody Maker* magazine on 23 April 1966, Brian called himself the youngest alcoholic in London. He struggled with mental health issues, and wisely sought psychiatric help, which their parents would have needed decades earlier, yet again they went for their pride, despite probably knowing that "Pride goes before destruction, a haughty spirit before a fall." (Proverbs 16:18).

Brian also had problems with aggression, because he had an enormous amount of pain he did not know how to deal with, and he had not learnt how to express anger in a socially acceptable and reasonable way. Anger is perfectly normal and it must not be suppressed, but adults raging with their anger out of control was the only way he had learnt anger was expressed. How was he supposed to master something which he had not seen or learnt the basics of at home? That is what parents are meant to teach their children by setting an example.

He also engaged in risky and erratic behaviour that others thought was simply crazy. One of such displays was a boat trip in the USA in November 1965, when the Stones were on their second American tour of 1965; they had a spring and autumn tour in North America that year. One afternoon, emerging from the room he was sharing with Pallenberg, Brian wanted to have a motor boat ride. After locating a boat hire, Brian got into a boat, pointed it out to sea and continued onward until he ran out of petrol. Others had to chase after him and tow his boat back, and they were not pleased. But Brian, apparently nonchalant and unaware of the risk to which he had exposed himself, thought the incident was incredibly funny.[2]

Why do that? Because he was a person with issues, and his parents had not given him the attention he needed for positive things. We all need attention, but he had learnt to get it only when acting in unusual ways, so he was used to negative attention. It is, of course, far from ideal, but that was what he was used to, and he at least got some.

His relationships with women were a tangled web of misfortunes on each side. He sought love and found it, occasionally, but he was very mindful of not getting into a web where others would control him again. He was very determined to keep a safe distance without being tied down, but it so happens that women fall pregnant, when you have sex with them. Not necessarily every time, but the more often you do it in a short period of time, the higher the likelihood of an ensuing pregnancy. And Brian did it often enough, and a bit more, just to be on the safe side; a man does not want to miss an opportunity. On a certain level, he probably did not care. Why should he? Why would he? Nobody had cared about him, and he did not know what a loving relationship felt like. A healthy relationship involving care and respect was something he had not experienced, and he did not know how to last without aggression and drama longer than the time-span between parental outbursts at home. And Brian witnessed them, and they were horrendous.

Incredibly, Brian's parents locked him out in the street before Christmas 1960, when he was only 18 years old. There was no prior warning, and the age of majority was 21 until it was reduced by Family Law Reform Act in 1969. The rest of the family had gone to Wales for the Christmas holiday, and his parents committed this vicious act of ill will towards their own child in the middle of the winter, leaving him to fend for himself with no place to go and no food on offer. Things had been bad before that, with Brian temporarily working in an old quarry, to help to lay the foundation of Crich Tramway Village not far from Sheffield. Of course, such manual labour was not acceptable to his parents, for which reason Brian liked it even better, but the matter had further soured things at home. However, there was no excuse for what Brian's parents did. Only a cold and heartless person would do that ever.

Things came to a head on 22 December 1960, when Brian and his girlfriend Pat had planned an evening out to celebrate her 16th birthday on that day. Brian and she went together to Brian's home, for him to change his clothes before going out. It came as a total surprise to him to find the house standing empty in darkness with all doors and windows of the house locked up. Brian did not have a key, which his parents were undoubtedly aware of, and after searching for a way in, Brian broke in through a window. But before that, he had found outside a suitcase with a note from his parents. The note let him know that the others had gone to Wales for Christmas. And no, the parents did not cut their Christmas holiday short to return to their son they had deserted in the street.

No matter how you look at it, it was an evil thing to do. Heartless, loveless and as cold as ice. What makes it worse is that the parents did not act on an impulse or in the heat of the moment, but they planned it with every intent to do it. That they continued to stay in Wales and sing Christmas carols to celebrate the arrival of their King of Kings is absurd and sickening. That they did not call Brian to apologize profusely and say they had acted like morons has no justification. There is no point in Lewis Jones writing to Brian in April 1964 that he had done what he thought was the best at the time. How can abandoning your child be the best for him ever? That is utter rubbish. Then again, it is unlikely they ever apologized to him for the harm they had done to him. 'I apologize for the wrong I did to you' or 'I love you' where expressions outside the vocabulary of Brian's parents.

In July 1962, Brian, now living in London, phoned his parents in Cheltenham, after months of no contact, to say he wanted to talk to them about a band he was starting. He then went to see them a few days later. Their meeting went well, and Brian told his parents he had started his group called the Rollin' Stones, and he was wanting to become a jazz musician. Brian's father, the traditional patriarchal head of the family, said that this meeting marked the complete and lasting reconciliation in their relationship.[3]

But we do not know what was said between father and son, and one saying there was reconciliation does not mean the feeling was mutual. It could just be that it was what Lewis Jones was feeling, and more than anything it is likely to have meant that he was not going to actively run down Brian anymore. But there is nothing to suggest that problems were discussed and worked out, which is the only way to a reconciliation. Reconciliation does not mean that one party decides not to continue dysfunctional conduct. It means that problems are discussed, responsibility is laid where it belongs, apologies are made and accepted, and then both move on in an improved relationship. Such things take time, and they do not happen in a one-off chat over a cup of tea; they may take years to be worked through by both parties.

There are no grounds to suggest that any factual reconciliation took place between Brian and his father. For that to happen, Lewis would have had to, if not accept, then at least acknowledge and respect Brian's version of the past events. How likely could it be that Lewis Jones, out of the blue, would acknowledge his own wrong-doing in his behaviour without making excuses for it? How likely is it that he could ever have apologized to Brian for being cold, overly dominating and unloving towards his son, if he was the patriarchal head of the family? That Brian was emotionally neglected was the truth, but how likely is it that Lewis Jones was capable of accepting his son's version of the past? There is no way in the world any of it happened between Brian and his father. For that to be true, Lewis Jones would have had to become another person, but the distance Brian's parents kept from their grandchildren after Brian's passing is diametrically opposed to that suggestion. People can change and do change, but only if they want to. There is no credibility to the assumption that all of a sudden Lewis Jones, who had always been right and known everything better than Brian, would miraculously have developed a new personality. For a way forward, a remarkable change would have had to take place. Otherwise there would only be another layer of pretence:

Unspoken rule No 1 Father and Brian have reconciled.

Unspoken rule No 2 Everybody knows it is not true.

Unspoken rule No 3 Everyone will pretend it is true.

And then the vicious circle starts again.

Around two years later, Brian's father went to see one of the Rolling Stones concerts in Bristol on 10 May 1964, on which occasion he apparently stood backstage smiling with pride. Again, the parents went to see the Stones in concert in Cheltenham ca. three months later, on 10 September 1964, and no rift seemed apparent between Brian and his mother and father. Against this background one would believe everything was running smoothly between Brian and his parents, although we are still talking about appearances in public only. Problems do not disappear by telling others they are gone, and private life is always behind closed doors.

The above dates are important, because they cast direct light on Brian and his parents' relationship. Between the dates of July 1962, May 1964 and September 1964 another baby Brian had with a girlfriend announced his arrival, and the baby boy was born in June 1964. After the young lovebirds found out about the news, her parents wanted them to tell his parents as well. One can only imagine how distressing it must have been for Brian to just think of the unavoidable spectacle of red hot anger dished out at Brian in his parents' front room. Regardless, Brian and his girlfriend got on their way to share the news, and a mile or two from the parents' house Brian had to stop the car, because he suddenly had a vicious asthma attack and he could not breathe. The prospect of facing his parents with more baby news was too horrifying for him. And he was not wrong: the occasion turned out so unbearable that he did not manage to break the news at all, so he sent a letter with the news to his parents afterwards. The response was the same verbal onslaught as before.[4]

But there cannot have been a reconciliation in May 1962, if Brian was as distressed as that about just facing his parents in late 1963. If his parents continued to be upset about a pregnancy Brian had caused in the past, especially after an alleged 'complete and lasting reconciliation' over a year earlier, there cannot have been a reunion between father and son in 1962. And the truth remained the incontestable and sad one: Brian's parents did not accept him the way he was, be it warts and all, but continued their abysmal behaviour. How can you say that love your child, if you do not accept his choices?

Lewis Jones wrote another letter to his son Brian on 1 April 1964. It was April Fool's Day. In it he called himself an intolerant father and said that he hoped Brian could try a little to forgive him, which was a tall order, to say the least. Brian was then 22, and his father had spent 22 years suffocating him emotionally with great success. He also asked Brian not to think he was writing the letter only because Brian had turned out successful. It is not known if Brian believed him or not, but the letter does coincide with Brian's fame growing and the Stones' finance blossoming. It would be easier to think Lewis Jones was sincere, if he and Brian's mother had stayed in contact with Brian's children after his passing. But all there was for a contact was the odd letter to one or the other of the grandchildren a few times, which makes you think that the grandchildren were not good enough just the way they were; they had no social status being children out of wedlock, and being children, no money, of course. Be that as it may, Lewis and Louisa Jones were not devoting grandparents enjoying their grandchildren's company, which casts doubt on the sincerity of Lewis Jones' letter on April Fool's Day in 1964.

Brian's past in Cheltenham with his cold parents devoid of affection for Brian is directly related to Brian's emotional collapse after Morocco in March 1967. His insecurities and lack of insight into what healthy relationships were like were the precursors of all his troubled relationships, whether friendships or love affairs. That is because people from dysfunctional families are likely to repeat what they have experienced, and they enter into relationships a more balanced person would not get involved in. Yes, the incidents in Cheltenham before 1962 and the ones in Morocco in March 1967 were chronologically apart, but Brian had the same feelings originally instilled and ignored by his parents; emotional destruction does not expire with time, unless it is addressed and repaired to the extent possible. The disaster and destruction that hit Brian in his last two years was a consequence of all the hurt he had experienced before, because we cannot erase the past and pretend it did not exist, and then successfully continue as nothing ever happened.

Morocco in March 1967 heralded the darkest time in Brian's life and led to his mental and physical destruction. The deadly blow was dealt by the only woman he apparently ever loved, Anita Pallenberg, who abandoned him after starting a relationship with Keith Richards. Pallenberg (1942–

2017) herself does not seem to have been a balanced person, and her devotion to the occult and black magic, combined with a heavy drug use, appear to have culminated in an anti-social personality with low, if any, inter-personal skills. But the trip entourage, which also included Mick Jagger, left Brian in Morocco and returned to England in various ways during his temporary absence from the hotel. Brian did not have an inkling of it going to happen. He always had on-going issues with abandonment and rejection, both of which he suffered from since early childhood. However, it seems that privacy borders have never been much respected among pop stars and other celebrities, and free improvisation, shall we say, continues to be the norm. It had happened to Brian before, when he was briefly seeing a young star known as Twinkle in 1965. Her real name was Lynn Ripley (1948–2015), and she told *Daily Mail* in 2015 that Jagger had ordered Brian to hand over Twinkle, to which Brian objected and said he considered the matter her decision. Twinkle said she stayed put.[5]

That Brian was left behind on his own in Morocco was callous, brutal and inexcusable treatment of another human being. The other Stones members, and there were three of them as well as some inside aids, one of them being Tom Keylock, only made matters worse by not standing up for Brian. Not at the time and not ever, when Brian was still alive. Indeed, while those others were not present in Morocco at the time and did not directly participate in what those involved did, they did not help Brian either. They did not object to the way in which Brian was treated. Instead, they let him down knowingly, wilfully and with an intent to do so. There is precious little merit in writing later about how badly Brian was treated, when they had every opportunity to stand up not only for Brian, but for fairness and justice in general. Speaking up now is better late than never, but while it may ease bangs of conscience for those who did not do it at the time, it does nothing to help Brian, so best not be too noble about that. They all abandoned Brian in their ways, and none of them did anything to help Brian. He was deserted in the lonely darkness of the heart-broken who have nowhere to go.

The long periods of depression and hopelessness lonely Brian sank in were a combination of sorrow, bitter hurt and disappointment, and the following few years of his life were dark and desolate, like a landscape of emotional permafrost swept with cold winds. After a long darkness, a vagrant ray of sunshine will bring forth the odd blossom of white arctic cotton, until a tuft of blossoms bursts out with half a degree of warmth in the air.

Gradually, Brian picked up the pieces of what had been, now reshaped with the frozen water drops that melted and refroze on a sudden cold night of despair, when the hurt hit him again. But just as life will eventually re-emerge wherever rays of sun touch the frozen wasteland, he started to rebuild his life again, piece by piece. Yet the abandonment, combined with his painful and difficult childhood, had its disastrous consequences for Brian; he was mortally wounded and could not recover. The others had effectively taken his music, his group and the woman he was besotted with.

In fact, he never was back himself, says his father, who continues on the matter on the BBC Radio 4 programme *A Story of our Time in* 1971 as follows, with *italics* marking the emphasis in his voice:

"What I *firmly* believe was that the turning point in his life was when he lost *the only girl* he ever really loved.

I think this was a *very* severe blow to him. He changed suddenly and alarmingly from a bright and enthusiastic young man to a quiet and morose, and inward looking young man, so much so that when his mother and I saw him for the first time some months after this…happening, we were quite shocked by the change in his appearance, and in our opinion he was never the same boy again…. I am *quite convinced*, and I'll *always be* convinced that was the turning point in Brian's life, rather than the pop scene generally."

At a London court hearing on 12 December 1967, Brian's defence presented that he had become suicidal. The hearing was an appeal from his drug conviction a couple of months earlier in October. Much to everyone's relief, Brian won his appeal. But the following day, 13 December 1967, Brian's chauffeur Brian Palastanga found him unconscious in his flat and took him to hospital, thereby saving his life. Was it a suicide attempt? Impossible to conclude either way. But Brian had already tried to commit suicide earlier in 1967, between late May and October. On that occasion he was driving down the London Embankment with Palastanga, and when Palastanga stopped the car momentarily, Brian attempted to jump into the Thames. On the balance of probabilities, it does look like Brian Palastanga saved his employer's life twice.

Sons of controlling Mothers

The Jones family was one with the traditional family system of a wise, capable and knowledgeable father earning money outside the home, and a rosy, loving mother flourishing as the homemaker in a happy domestic idyll, where the smell of daily baking greeted a visitor at the door.

She was meant to be caring and loving, taking care of her children and family. She was meant to be a mother who makes the family home a welcoming and nurturing place for her children. An important task it is today as much as ever, and an incredibly important task it was in the post-war era with too many lost or injured in the horrors of the war. Men returning home and those welcoming them back were just as much hoping for the comfort and safety of a loving home. It was bitter for families who had lost a dear family member, and the pain was felt every day. Making a home was important, and life was moving onward, as best it could. And Louisa Jones undoubtedly wanted a good home for her children, and preferably a Christian one to boot.

But she had problems of her own, so much so that she could not offer to Brian what he needed. She probably did not offer to others at home what they needed either, including her husband. What Brian needed enormously and never received at home, consequently having problems with it in adulthood, was protection and feeling of being safe and loved. Learning those basics happens in the first few years of our life, and if we then learn to be safe in moments of stress we experience in our baby years, bearing in mind that babies, too, experience stress, we will have the ability to deal with stressful situations as adults. Any baby is likely to have problems with having his baby needs met, if the mother is severely burdened with her own issues from her childhood, which probably was the case with Brian's mother. It would explain the emotional coldness displayed to Brian, unless she was a person with no ethics and a purposeful intent to harm Brian, which is unlikely to have been the case. Brian's mother was not responsible for having turned out a dysfunctional, controlling mother. That was the responsibility and failure of her parents. But what she was responsible for was continuing the vicious circle and not seeking help for herself. She would have known she was feeling very unwell for no particular reason, and it was her responsibility to deal with her own unwellness.

How detrimental the domestic situation is likely to have been for little Brian is highlighted in research studies on the mother-baby relationship. Babies need a loving, smiling maternal face, and as early as at the minimal age of four months, they are more distressed during a maternal face that does not smile than during physical separation. This suggests that a mother's emotional unavailability is more troubling for the baby than the mother's physical absence.[6]

The more time you spend with your little one, the better it is. Brian's mother had time, being at home, but then the tragedy of the first daughter Pamela passing away hit the whole family hard. Brian, born in February 1942, was around 18 months old when Pamela was born in October 1943, and when she passed away in October 1945, Brian was only 3 years and 6 months old. He was a toddler badly in need of caring and nurturing. If a child at this age does not receive the nurturing needed, he cannot develop mentally as he normally would. As said before, we need love and safety to balance out moments of stress in our first years, but Brian would only have experienced more stress with the burden he would have sensed his parents were going through with Pamela in the two years of her short life. Brian would have remained confused, badly in need of safety and comfort, and he probably cried himself to sleep at night. His mother was not only burdened with her history from the past, but also with what was unfolding with Brian's sister Pamela. She was a young child, and the only treatment for leukaemia until 1948–1949 were blood transfusions and some antibacterial agents that would kill bacteria, fungi and algae, and looking back from the modern day, it was not much at all. In 1948, researchers at the Boston Children's Hospital reported that aminopterin produced remissions in about one third of children with acute leukaemia. It was a tremendous result and a monumental step forward in the field of chemotherapy.

But 1948 was too late for little Pamela, and as usual, her leukaemia ran its usual course with a life expectancy of a few months from the time of the diagnosis. The only help her parents and doctors could offer were pain killers for the little one. It is not known if she spent time in hospital or at home and what the arrangements were around her, but whatever was happening in that regard, the parents were grieving and focused on Pamela, which invariably resulted in far less attention to little Brian.

Babies come into the world totally dependent on adults for survival. They also arrive equipped with characteristics behaviours to enable them to get attention and care they need: they smile, squeal, laugh and scream to get the carer's attention. It is most important that the baby has a number one carer, and that is usually the mother, because the baby needs to establish a firm relationship with her and she carries the milk bar in ideal temperature. But it does not suffice for the mother only to be there; she must be there in a nurturing way. The nurturing presence of the number one carer is the way babies reach development stages they need to go through, to develop a solid sense of self, trust in others, and basic functions of cause and effect. While every infant is different and babies' abilities to respond to stimuli varies, the mother must provide the necessary stimuli and emotional warmth in her interactions with the baby. It is the mother's and her baby's first language in which they communicate. The mother must be emotionally available for the baby's emotional availability to develop. A mother and her baby are partners in the child's steps of socialization outcomes. The basic behavioural agenda involved in the socialization process is shared by all mothers and infants, and it unfolds automatically, as longs as the mother is not dysfunctional.

Brian's mother was not much good with expressing her feelings, and the times before Pamela's passing must have been very difficult in the Jones household. It seems Brian's mother was emotionally absent at best of times, and during the first three years of his life, Brian probably became emotionally damaged already. And tragedy in the household would only continue after Pamela's passing, because the grief his mother must have felt was enormous. It may be that other family members from Wales came to help; Brian's parents both had siblings. Their support would have comforted everyone, but if they were cut from the same cloth as Brian's parents, embracing and words of comfort were unlikely to decorate and enhance daily conversations. Yet little Brian was starving for comfort, emotional safety and feelings of being loved. He was not able to shelve those needs in his little being until the adults had come to terms with the loss of his sister, because such needs cannot be put on hold until a mother finds a more suitable time to deal with them.

Further, in the 1940s nobody had coined the term 'quality time', which is a modern day pretentious idealisation of the too small amount of time parents spend with their children these days; they call it 'quality time' to disguise the fact that they are not spending enough time with their children. Not spending enough time with your children would not be a good thing at all. In that case you might as well admit your parenting is lacking and who wants to do that, but if we decide what little time you spend with your child is 'quality time', then the measly amount of it does not matter; you can substitute lack of quantity with quality, right? Not so fast, because the obvious fundamental problem is that the child does not know when you are spending 'quality time' and when you are spending 'crappy and forgettable time' with them. In children's world time is time, and they just want to spend time with you. Giving it a fancy name is not going to make one iota of a difference to what you are doing, except you feel better about yourself, which was the point of the exercise in the first place, so pat yourself on the back, and might as well press a reward sticker on your forehead, too, for the dork you are being.

Brian's mother, like any other mother in her situation, felt intense disbelief and denial of what was happening to Pamela. And those feelings were exacerbated with her inability to change what was happening to Pamela during the months of her sickness, as well as Pamela's inevitable passing away. Her sadness was overwhelming, perhaps to the extent that daily chores became a challenge, because there did not seem to be a positive future ahead without pain. There is no doubt that she felt intense anger and feelings of bitterness and unfairness over a life left unfulfilled and her God letting her down. It is not unusual for mothers to resent the healthy children they have, or other people with healthy children, when they are faced with the daunting challenge to look after a terminally ill child. Whatever she felt in the months before and after Pamela's passing, she would have been a sombre person to have around, if not anti-social; sometimes we feel it is better to lick our wounds alone and try to recover in isolation. She probably felt nobody could truly understand how she felt, and she was right; her family were unique human beings, like we all are. But there was her little son, who could only watch the way his mother's distress manifested itself from his point of view. The little boy badly needed love and protection. He needed to be touched, cuddled, kissed and go through positive feelings; he was too young to understand and communicate about such profound matters. He needed his mommy.

Effectively, Brian's mother was emotionally absent from Brian in those months and years. It is likely that she felt depressed and exhausted, or perhaps somewhat numb from her emotional overload, even if she did not want to show it. Yet it was there, and she was feeling it, because it does not disappear or evaporate only because you are uncomfortable with it. It is rather the opposite: the more uncomfortable you feel about your feelings, life situations and your inability to discuss your feelings, the greater your problems will grow. In saying she was emotionally absent from Brian, we are saying she was not fully present in general, and she was absent from Brian's emotional life in particular. From the child's point of view, there was precious little difference in whether his mother was not willing to discuss her feelings and approach Brian the way he needed it, or whether she did not have the ability to do so. It was an incredibly bad situation for Brian, and he was emotionally neglected. Apparently, Brian was told that Pamela had been sent away for misbehaviour and he would also be sent away, if he did not behave. What kind of decent person would do that? What kind of a parent would do that, or say it to his or her child?

Brian needed a physically and emotionally present mother in order to develop a solid sense of self-esteem and security. When a mother neglects a son emotionally, he is likely to suffer insecurity issues involving avoidance of close relationships and general fearfulness of being abandoned. Brian did fear being abandoned and he had been threatened with being abandoned by his parents. It then happened to him a number of times, and when he was abandoned in Morocco, he was abandoned by several people in one go. They were people whom he trusted and whom he thought to be his friends. He was abandoned again and again, just as he was abandoned by his mother, when she turned inwards to try and cope with her own grief.

No mother can be a good mother in the meaning of providing her child with what he needs, if she is not emotionally available. You cannot have any relationship if you do not show feelings and let the other one close, regardless who the other person is. It may be your child, your partner or anyone else you want a close relationship with, but in order to have healthy relationship, you must show your emotions, good and bad, in a meaningful way. A part of it is getting vulnerable and taking risks with showing emotions, but if you do not give you cannot receive, and in a relationship with your child, you damage the child. The relationship becomes unhealthy and turns toxic; you become a toxic mother to your child. That happened to little Brian.

An overbearing or toxic mother, depending on what term you wish to use, results in children being more likely to suffer from lower psychological well-being, and the likelihood of medication for anxiety and depression increases. Those children simply have a more difficult time adjusting to life as adults, which results in poorer mental health. A toxic stay-at-home mother in particular, which was the case in Brian's home, creates a negative and poisonous home environment with unhealthy interactions and relationships, which damage the child's sense of self and the child's views of relationships with others. Such a child ends up with relationships becoming unhealthy and distorted, because he not only lacks a healthy sense of identity, but he also does not learn how to interact with

others in a reasonable and balanced way. The child is likely to develop problems with self-control, regulating his emotions and running social relationships. And Brian Jones displayed all those symptoms in his adult conduct. Not because he was bad, but because he had a very troubled background, and he was not responsible for it. A child is never responsible for anything his mother did or does, and he does not need to, indeed he must not, put his mother's feelings before his owns. He is responsible for himself, and the mother must be responsible for herself and everything she did, or did not.

Had Brian's mother raised her son to be emotionally intelligent, a term used for people who are comfortable with themselves and expressing their feelings, Brian would have had a different life. He would have been confident in his own skin and would not have been so fearful of committing himself in a relationship.

Sons of Controlling Fathers

Franz Kafka (July 1884–June 1924) was born an Austrian citizen in the Kingdom of Bohemia in Austria-Hungary, and he died of tuberculosis aged 40 in Austria. His father Hermann Kafka was a wealthy businessman and a man with a strong sense of a self-entitlement to make commands and expect others to comply: things had to be his way, and Franz' mother did not object. Franz group up insecure and fearful of his father, and his childhood was lonely. He was ordered around by his father, and he felt unloved and did not think he was good enough; he was a prolific writer of books with a dark undertone. Sadly, he was also tormented with intense self-doubt, and he burnt over 80% of what he wrote, because he felt none of it was good enough. Which is also a huge loss for the literary world.

Franz Kafka never married, although he was engaged several times and was constantly seeing new women, including prostitutes; he was not faithful to any woman in his life but entertained any relationship whenever he felt like it. Reiner Stach, a Kafka biographer, says that Kafka's life was full of incessant womanizing and that he was filled with fear of sexual failure.[7] Kafka had several relationships with women in his lifetime, and Max Brod, another biographer on Kafka, described him as 'tortured by sexual desire'.[8] Kafka visited brothels for prostitutes for most of his adult life, and he was keenly interested in pornography. He remained an insecure person of great creativity and intelligence, with an excellent command for expressions in his eloquent use of language, and he became a world renowned artist with prolific production and unique, intellectual interests. – Rather like Brian Jones, was he not?

Kafka's father Hermann wanted to know why his son maintained that he was afraid of his father, and Franz Kafka wrote a letter to his father to answer the question. The letter became ca. 100 pages long, and was later published as a book with the title *Brief an meinen Vater* (Letter to My Father). It is a tragic story of a traumatic childhood, and he only managed to write it at the age of 36. Sadly, as it turned out, Kafka gave the letter to his mother, for her to pass it onto his father. It may be that his mother Julie considered giving it to her husband, but decided to return it to her son unread. The result was that Franz Kafka never had an opportunity to answer his father's question, and father Hermann and his son Franz became totally estranged. They remained aliens to each other in the life they shared daily, which undoubtedly aggrieved them both. But father Hermann would not deal with the matter. – This is how Franz Kafka begins his letter to his father, in English translation:

Dearest Father,

You asked me recently why I maintain I am afraid of you. As usual, I was unable to think of any answer to your question, partly for the very reason I am afraid of you, and partly because the explanation of the grounds for this fear would mean going into far more details than I would ever approximately keep in mind while talking. And if I now try to give you an answer in writing, it will still be very incomplete …

It is easy to see, even without reading further, that the matter was enormous for him and weighed heavily on his shoulders. Like with Franz Kafka, Brian's relationship with his father was traumatic, laden with hostility between father and son, and the son was bound to develop a negative self-image; if the son does not receive positive feedback from the father, there is no foundation for stages of positive development to take place. Self-image is not a given children have at birth. Rather, it consists of stages of construction over years, and it starts very early in the first few months.

Equally, like Kafka, Brian lived most of his life in the physical protection and comfort of his family. Brian never lacked things material in his childhood home. But physical, material and financial safety do most certainly not translate into mental well-being without distress and trauma: psychological distress can be just as traumatising as physiological distress. Brian was psychologically abused by his father through the oppression he experienced. As discussed before, Brian feared seeing his parents to tell them about Linda's pregnancy in 1964. He felt more than fear: it was real horror. There is no room for the potential argument that perhaps his fear of his father was imaginary and not real, because he was so fearful that he had an asthma attack.

Trauma cannot be defined from outside. The criterion of whether it is real or alleged with no foundation is the person's experience and understanding of what happened. Trauma and distress are always subjective, and there can be no standard that fits all; quite understandably, there never could be, because everyone is different and circumstances are different. If you are genuinely telling how you felt and say you felt oppressed, then that is the truth. Brian went repeatedly through overwhelming experiences that went beyond his ability to cope, and the world his father represented was threating and outside his abilities to deal with.

Brian needed the presence of a loving father for the construction of his self-image from early on, and he could only develop a positive self-image in the company of a secure bond with his parents, mother and father alike. Systematic rejection and criticism were what he was dealt with, and positives were absent. His father was particularly important for the development of Brian's self-esteem and self-confidence as a man. He needed to get it from his father, because he needed the male model for it. Boys crave warm affection from their fathers, even if the father is not capable of providing it. The child's need for it will not disappear; instead, damage will occur. If the son has an egocentric, competitive father as Brian did, the son will end up feeling like they are never good enough to gain the father's approval. And Brian became like that; all he was seeking was acknowledgement from his father that he was good enough. He became agonized with restlessness, anxiety, depression and issues with aggression.

Boys also learn their traits of sexuality and masculinity from their fathers, which reflects on their role in the lives of the women they are going to meet. What is decisive is how the father interacts with the mother, and how boys learn about sexuality and the standards of behaviour. We know nothing about the privacy of Brian's parents, but it being just another part of their lives, it cannot have been much different from other areas of their lives. It is reasonable to say it did not contain conduct of strong affection, be it mental of physical by nature. Brian was probably left on his own to find his way into information and behaviour regarding puberty and sexual relationships, and his experiences from his time at school suggest an inquisitive and creative mind in that regard. His father did not display a positive and healthy understanding of his son's physical development and psychological maturing, yet it was essential for Brian to become confident about himself and his sexuality.

Whether we are happy with our partner or miserably attached through codes of 'must not' is typically a reflection of the type of bond that our parents nurtured between them. How much importance our fathers place on job security, high income and professional reputation factor into a child's career choices, decisions and achievements, or lack thereof. It was very important for Brian that his father would acknowledge Brian's efforts and achievements and that he did well, despite going against what his father had in mind for him. It is not known if and how his father expressed his wishes for Brian's own family-to-be, but Brian's known comments to his father involved around his achievements with the Rolling Stones. If Lewis Jones expressed any wishes regarding Brian's potential family, the example he had set through his conduct in the family home was nothing Brian wanted to follow and repeat; Brian was at a loss, how to be a positive and loving father. Becoming a father is something men learn by integrating what they learn fatherhood to mean, and that is the way that fatherhood was acted out by their own father at home. But with Brian, the way fatherhood was acted out at home essentially destroyed him.

Had Brian's father had a close relationship with his son, and had he not been deeply dysfunctional, he would have had a powerful influence on instilling adult ethics and values on his son by displaying those ethics and values in his own conduct. That, in turn, would have resulted in a more mature inner moral compass in Brian, as it were, as well as created a more balanced maturity in him, to use as a resource in his adult choices, decisions made and actions chosen between him and other people. While a loving and nurturing mother is very important to a newborn and infant, and will remain so throughout the child's life, the father becomes increasingly more important to the son as the son grows older. The son learns to be a man through the conduct of his father. A loving mother naturally encourages this relationship, and the relationship between the three is a nurturing one, resulting the son gaining a sense of independent identity and the parents learning to step back to let go, and just love their adult son in action in his own life. Young Brian should have learnt from his father what being responsible, ethical, caring, and appropriate in a relationship mean, but he did not have the opportunity to do so. Teenaged Brian watched how his father treated women, valued his work and related to Brian himself as well as his sisters, and that was the way he learnt to conduct himself in his roles to other people.

Brian remained yearning for a loving relationship with his father. It became a repressed longing not expressed, and undoubtedly his father felt the same way about his son. But it became an unexpressed one, because verbalizing it would have meant having to deal with anger, rejection and intense sadness accumulated over the years, and Brian turned out to loathe himself instead. Just as was the case with Franz Kafka, who wrote to his father that the hostility his father showed against him in his childhood turned Franz against himself in his adulthood. It resulted in a burden of fear towards his father, weakness and self-contempt. Brian's life story entails the same turbulence of self-hatred Kafka experienced in his misery. Franz Kafka and Brian both had their minds haunted by the image of a hostile father disapproving of his son. Brian was always trying to live up to his father's expectations, and he was undoubtedly struggling just as much with what burdened Kafka, as Kafka expressed in his letter:

> "What was always incomprehensible to me was your total lack of feeling for the suffering and shame you could inflict on me with your words and judgments."

The only area of life where the respective fathers of Franz Kafka and Brian Jones failed to haunt their sons was their sexuality. It became an arena of gaining control over another person, as happens in sexual encounters: we have the power to thrill the other and prove ourselves as capable of doing it. It is not a power game as such, but power to excite and satisfy are always present in the contact. Perhaps that was the reason why both Franz and Brian seemingly over-indulged in physiological pleasures, although underneath there was obviously sorrow. Feeling competent to give sexual pleasure and factually doing so gave them both a feeling of power over circumstances; usually it was the circumstances defeating them in other fields of life, and they never felt they were good enough.

Now, let us return to the question: Did Brian's parents love him? It is noteworthy that before Brian left Cheltenham for London in 1960, his parents further soured relationships at home by causing a drift between Brian and his sister Barbara. Apparently they were close as children, whatever 'close' ever meant in the Jones household, but as Brian grew older and began his rebellion in his teens, the parents decided to 'protect' Barbara from Brian's 'bad' influence. As the parents desired, it created a schism between the brother and sister, and Brian felt even more alienated at home. With that in mind, it is hard to argue that the parents treated their children with an equal amount of love or affection. Parents turning siblings against each other is always particularly unethical and mean. It was totally selfish and heartless of the Jones parents not only towards Brian, but also his sister. The parents did not act in the interest of Barbara in the least; they drove the siblings apart in their attempt to make at least one child turn out the way they wanted their children to be, and they did it for their own needs only and not for those of Barbara. That parents intentionally turn siblings against each other is callous in the highest and extremely cruel. It seems incomprehensible how Lewis and Louisa Jones managed to sleep in their home, considering the emotional pain they kept inflicting on their children.

Several years after Brian's passing, his father commented on the painful relationship between Brian and his parents with a peculiar acknowledgement that while Brian in time proved his parents wrong, Lewis Jones gives him credit for never telling his father that he had told him so. Brian only said 'Well, I haven't done so bad, Dad, have I'?[9]

The words are very strange, and an objective and reasonable person would find it troublesome to understand why Lewis would praise and applaud Brian for not saying 'I told you so'. What could be praiseworthy of him not saying 'I told you so'? Nothing at all, of course, because it would be perfectly normal and reasonable that a person who has been wronged would say to his wrong-doer 'I told you so', when the light has finally gone up in the mind of the wrong-doer. But as always before, and years after the reconciliation Lewis alleged happened in 1962, the issue continued to be Lewis himself. Not Brian, and not what Brian did. It was the same old song of Lewis Jones not being able to tolerate being wrong and Brian being right, because Lewis was always right and that is the way it was. It was always Brian running around and looking after his father's feelings, trying to avoid stepping on those sensitive toes. That is what Lewis was giving Brian credit for: that he did not say to his father 'I told you so', meaning 'I told you then and I was right', because Lewis Jones' pride and warped ideas of his infallibility were at stake, and Lewis would not have welcomed being told he was wrong all along. He would not have accepted it, which Brian undoubtedly knew. – So much for the alleged reconciliation years earlier: happy-happy la-la.

There are events also after 2 July 1969 that may answer at least to some extent the question if Lewis and Louisa loved their son Brian, but one cannot know the thoughts of another person ever. Brian's parents attended his funeral on 10 July 1969 and looked sombre and sad. They had wished for a minimum of attention to the occasion, and it is good their wish was not granted to them; Brian deserved to be remembered and respected by the large crowd of people who attended and honoured him with the seas of flowers that were brought to Cheltenham cemetery. Indeed, his parents looked like sombre and grieving people do. Then again, everyone usually does at a funeral, and you cannot assess the depth of somebody's love, or lack thereof, by appearances; how could that be possible? Undoubtedly, they felt a loss and were confused by the suddenness of the events in early July. They did cry and the atmosphere was dark, but tears do not automatically mean love, because remorse, hay fever, dust, cat allergy and guilt can make you cry, too. But are you then crying for the deceased or feeling sorry for yourself and your loss? They also rejected the request from Alexis Korner, Brian's good friend, supporter and mentor, to attend Brian's funeral, alleging that Korner's presence would be inappropriate: the parents were obviously still not accepting Brian's choices for friendships. As for tombstones: when their first daughter passed away in 1945, the parents chose a grave stone with the words 'in affectionate remembrance', and around 25 years later they only felt affection, but not love. Or if they did feel love, they either chose not to say so or had psychological barriers preventing them from saying so, which does occur with dysfunctional parents.

To answer the question, please do not hasten to triumphantly affirm 'of course they did'! Because parents do not automatically love their children, and some parents more or less hate their children, or one of them, although that is a result of their own psychological problems badly needing attention yet unlikely to receive any ever. But, and importantly, it is not at all self-explanatory that parents love their children.

Love feels like love, and those who have received it, know what it feels like. If someone says he loves you but you do not feel loved, the feeling shared is unlikely to be love. If someone says he loves you but they cause you hurt and emotional pain, it is definitely not love. Because when you love someone you give them what they need to shine and blossom. That is love, and it is always about the other person, and never about yourself. Parental love is no different, and it is always comforting and nourishing for the child. Further, love does not involve feelings only. It shows its presence in our actions, which cause feelings of love in another person. Such loving actions are in the heart of nurturing your child. Loving behaviour does not run down a child or another person, nor does it cause self-hatred or feelings of unworthiness in another person. Your parent loving you does not make you feel you are a bad person. Being loved makes you feel comfortable, welcome and accepted as the person you are. You feel safe in yourself and in your stable personality, and your feelings are those of warmth, joy and pleasure, because love always feels good.

You may find your answer to the question if Brian's parents loved him in their beloved New Testament; 1 Corinthians 13, as it was worded in *The Revised Standard Version* used in English parishes in the 1960s:

> If I speak with the tongues of men and of angels, but have not love, I am a noisy gong or a clanging cymbal. And if I have prophetic powers, and understand all mysteries and all knowledge, and if I have all faith, so as to remove mountains, but have not love, I am nothing. If I give away all I have, and if I deliver my body to be burned, but have not love, I gain nothing.
>
> Love is patient and kind; love is not jealous or boastful; it is not arrogant or rude. Love does not insist on its own way; it is not irritable or resentful; it does not rejoice at wrong, but rejoices in the right. Love bears all things, believes all things, hopes all things, endures all things.

Love never ends; as for prophesies, they will pass away; as for tongues, they will cease; as for knowledge, it will pass away. For our knowledge is imperfect and our prophecy is imperfect; but when the perfect comes, the imperfect will pass away.

When I was a child, I spoke as a child, I understood as a child, I reasoned as a child; when I became a man, I gave up childish things. For now we see in a mirror, dimly, but then face to face. Now I know in part; then I shall know fully, even as I have been fully understood.

So faith, hope, love, abide these three; but the greatest of these is love.

4
I Cannot Breathe!

'An asthmatic never knows if he will be able to breathe' were the words Marcel Proust (1871–1922), a French novelist and a literary critic used in a letter, to describe the despair he felt about his condition. He suffered from severe asthma throughout his life, and feared the coughing episodes so much that he stayed up at night. He rather kept to a hermit life than exposed himself to anything that might exacerbate his asthma. Proust's life was tormented with desperate attempts to find relief for his breathing problems, and he constantly feared not being able to breathe. But it turned out as if life played a cruel joke on Marcel's life: he developed pneumonia that destroyed his lungs, so he could not breathe and passed away at the age of 51. His father Adrien Proust was a medical doctor, who, like many of his contemporary medical colleagues, considered asthma a nervous affliction in the patient's mind. It was regarded as a mild and benign condition, affecting mostly neurotics of the privileged classes, which was highly offensive to Marcel, because he maintained he knew very well it was very real.

Similar problems burdened Brian throughout his life after he contracted croup at the age of four. It typically leaves a higher than average likelihood of developing bronchitis or asthma throughout one's life. But while it is not an automatic explanation for developing either, Brian, however, did develop asthma, and a nasty case of it to boot. So what is asthma, and what do authorities say about it?

Asthma is a lung condition in which your airways narrow and swell, and they may produce extra mucus. This can make breathing difficult and trigger coughing and wheezing when you breathe out, including shortness of breath. For some it is a minor nuisance, but there are those to whom it is a major problem interfering with daily activities. It may also lead to a life-threatening asthma attack. It cannot be cured, but its symptoms can be controlled medically. An asthma attack is always triggered with something internal or external to the patient's body, and the triggers are different with different people, although there are similarities.

Asthma has been known of for millennia, and herbal extracts were used to reduce the effect of the symptoms. Hippocrates (460–370 BC) coined the term *azein* in Greek, meaning *breathe hard*, and it was borrowed into English from the medieval Latin word *asma*, which in late Middle English (ca. 1400–1500) became *asthma*. During Alexander the Great's era in the 400s BC, the smoke of a herb called stramonium was used to 'relax the lungs', and in 50 AD, it was noticed that pollen caused breathing difficulty. During the Roman Empire (ca. until 450 AD), physicians noticed that inability to breathe without making noise and gasping occurred simultaneously, and physical exercise made the symptoms worse.

Remedies recommended over the centuries include ephedra extract, made from the ephedra plant's stems and leaves, combined with wine. It was considered excellent and safe until the early 2000s, when there was an accidental death of a person relying on natural remedies in the US. Harvard University Medical School then noticed that ephedra had unfortunate side effects, some of those being elevated heartbeat and blood pressure. It is certain that some 1900 years ago physicians were not aware of such issues. For an alternative treatment of owl's blood with wine you first had to catch the bird up the tree in a dark forest, so good luck with that. But since ephedra and owl's blood both had to be combined with wine in no particular proportion or quantity, it was more than likely that after a good dosage the patient was relaxed, dead or alive, and the coughing and wheezing had stopped.

Stress has long been recognised to be associated with asthma. Hippocrates found that to prevent an asthma attack 'the asthmatic should guard himself against his own anger.'[10] Maimonides (Moses ben Maimon, 1138–1204), a well-known medieval physician, wrote in his treatise on medical problems about asthma as well. He found that 'mental anguish, fear, mourning or distress' may cause asthma whereas 'gaiety and joy' which 'gladden the heart and stimulate the blood and mental activity' may have the opposite effect.[11] Closer to modern times, Henry Hide Salter (1823–1871) found that 'asthma is essentially, and with perhaps the exception of a single class of cases, exclusively a nervous disease; the nervous system is the seat of the essential pathological condition'[12]. Sir William Osler (1849–1919) went even further, and determined it was 'a neurotic affection'.

Sir William Osler, considered by some the father of modern medicine in the Western World, described asthma in his first (1892) edition of the textbook *Principles and Practice of Medicine* as follows (*italics* added to special points of interest:)

1. Spasm of the bronchial muscles
2. Swelling of the bronchial mucous membrane
3. A special form of *inflammation of the smaller bronchioles*
4. Having *many resemblances to hay fever*
5. The affection running in families.
6. *Often beginning in childhood* and sometimes lasting into old age.
7. *Bizarre and extraordinary variety of circumstances which at times induce a paroxysm*:
   a. Climate and atmosphere e.g. *hay, dust*, cat fur
   b. *Fright or violent emotion*
   c. Diet (overloading of the stomach) or certain foods
   d. Cold infection
8. Sputum is distinctive: rounded gelatinous masses ('*perles*') and Curschmann spirals & octahedral crystals of Leyden.

What is noticeable is that in the history of medicine, until the second half of the 20th century, asthma was predominantly viewed as a psychosomatic disorder in which emotional stress and imbalances in the nervous system were the key triggers of the onset of an attack.

But modern man knows best, and the technical world of the 20th century blossomed with medical improvements and laboratories, where everything could be measured precisely, including pollen and pollution. It was the century of petrol, steel, glass, stiletto heels, prolonged observation in cubicles, testing, medical companies and separation of particles. Researchers were able to dissect, subsect and micro sect. But no matter what they did about asthma, whether it was pollen from outside the patient's body or anxiety inside the patient's body, the airways were affected and the patient suffered an asthma attack, as described by Hippocrates some 2,500 years earlier. Researchers and professionals in their white coats had reason to consider new ways to proceed.

American psychosomatic medicine was born in the 1930s by Dr Helen Dunbar. According to this school of thought, emotional stimuli cause physiological effects, which cause illnesses. It was obviously a theory and rather difficult to prove either way. But it was the beginning of something new. The theory provided that repressed emotions emerged from the unconscious to target certain organs, producing psychosomatic disorders. To treat a medical problem, practitioners of psychosomatic medicine were required to search for psychological profiles characteristic of specific syndromes, which, of course, called for a very large database in an era of no computers. It is fair to consider the challenge unreasonable. The theory further expanded to the belief that many diseases were psychological in origin.

In the latter half of the 20th century, psychosomatic theories declined in popularity. It is understandable, considering that in 1967 researchers at the Children's Asthma Research Institute and Hospital in Denver discovered immunoglobulin E (IgE), which occurs naturally in the human body. Blood usually has small amounts of IgE antibodies, whereas higher amounts can be a sign that the body overreacts to allergens, which can lead to an allergic reaction. But it is a possibility and not an automatic formula; IgE levels can also be high, when the body is fighting an infection from a parasite or from some immune system conditions. Some of the diseases which cause the elevation of serum IgE levels include allergic rhinitis, asthma, atopic dermatitis, hives, parasitic diseases, acne and immune deficiencies.

But you can have a high level of IgE antibodies and not have asthma: the two do not correlate directly. However, the efficacy of biological therapies is evident only in patients who have experienced asthma exacerbations. Biological theories do not make asthma go away, nor do they explain why asthma occurs in the patient: the cause of asthma attacks remains to be established, and only the symptoms can be alleviated.

In the 1980s, it was widely accepted that with asthma the bronchial muscle (the breathing tube in layman's terms) is highly irritable, which makes asthmatics susceptible to a wide variety of external and psychological or physiological trigger factors. The level of bronchial muscle irritability determines the risk of a person developing an asthma attack, when exposed to trigger factors, be they external or internal ones for the patient. They can also be a combination of the two.

Psychosocial stress affects the nervous and immunological systems involved in the onset and exacerbation of various diseases, one of them being asthma. These psychological and stress-linked influences are typically related to major life events, such as reaching school age, employment, having a child, divorce and the like. Or dealing with an impossibly difficult situation at home, or starting a new job with full responsibility for the undertaking's future progress, which is what Brian had. Noticeably, all these involve interpersonal relationships. Such psychosocial stressors are often associated with the onset, exacerbation, or recurrence of asthma symptoms, and a close relation has been shown between emotion (anxiety, tension, anger, depression, etc.) and a flaring- up or a remission of asthma symptoms. A high rate of panic disorders has been reported for asthmatics, which can worsen asthmatic symptoms, and depression has been reported to be a risk factor for the death of asthmatic patients.

It is self-evident that Brian had a lot triggers for his asthma, which continued till the end of his short life. Yes, there was pollen in England, but he had psychological triggers since early childhood. Brian's class mate Roger described Brian's family as 'tension-ridden', and remarked on Brian's father never being content with what Brian did.[13] How do you live with a father who will not like you, unless you kill your own spirit? It is also worth bearing in mind that Brian's classmate was a person making observations from outside, and he did not participate in the Jones family private life behind closed doors.

Equally, the episode of Brian and his girlfriend Linda on their way to Cheltenham to tell his parents about the pregnancy sometime in late December 1963 or early 1964 is an account of a psychological trigger at work to produce a severe asthma attack. On that occasion, Brian had such a frightful asthma attack that they had to stop before reaching his parents' house. He was scared of his parents to the extent that he could not breathe, and he did not manage to tell his parents about the pregnancy during the visit. It was a psychosomatic asthma attack, originating in Brian's childhood trauma and triggered off later many times over in situations involving stress, anxiety and fear. Although his asthma attacks may have been triggered off by pollen as well, their real origins were in the painful family life Brian had to endure. He was suffocating and could not breathe.

And sadly, every time he went to visit Cheltenham after moving to London, he was back in square one, because his parents had not changed. They would not and did not. Every visit only deepened the schism between Brian and his parents, resulting in the flames of Brian's rebellion flaring up again, while inside he sank deeper in depression, despair and feelings of not being good enough. He was scared of his parents who kept rejecting their own son.

5
Why Brian Would Not Marry

Looking back at the known children Brian fathered, a tiny amount of consideration and an understanding of reality would provide a more realistic and truthful account of events, instead of listing his children born as the number of children he abandoned. Then again, it should not be surprising that the children known to be Brian's appear as a chronicle of life events he allegedly left behind without further ado. Somehow it is also incredibly appalling that there were 6 of them, which has been used to besmirch Brian after his death by ill-wishers who would find fault with him no matter what. There are millions of men or women with six children or more, so what is so abysmal about Brian having fathered 6 children or more? Apparently Mick Jagger has 8 children to 5 women and nobody minds, nor should they, but why the different standard for Brian?

There is no way of knowing how many children in the world have a Rolling Stone for a father. The guys had a global touring programme and an environmentally friendly sex life, if that be the term for it; it seems they were not particularly concerned about the consequences of their sexual encounters. In that regard they would be no different from other pop music performers, known for decades to brag about the number of the girls they had sex with. Adding to that the extent of their touring, which especially in the 1960s meant there were not going to be any paternity suits from outside the UK, the number of ensuing pregnancies would increase exponentially in the field of statistics. If there were statistics on the matter, that is. On the other hand, and considering how popular Brian was with women wanting sex with him, not that he wanted to disappoint any, the likelihood of a young girl falling pregnant on a weekend may have strongly been reduced by the Stones' busy days during the week, so that come Saturday, he may just have been shooting blanks. That would have been every girl's best chance to avoid pregnancy with Brian, because he did not like condoms, which he apparently told a young classmate of his using the words 'bareback's the best'[14]. Is there anyone who would not share his view?

According to Graham Ride, Brian's childhood friend from Cheltenham, Brian told him about Valerie being pregnant. At the same time, Brian also told Ride of another girl pregnant earlier, and the baby was given away.[15] That child would be Brian's first child, and it was with a schoolgirl referred to as Hope, which was not her real name. The baby is also mentioned by Nicholas Fitzgerald with whom Brian shared details of his past, and Fitzgerald mentions the matter a couple of times in his book. Fitzgerald was a good friend of Brian's since 1965 and a cousin of Tara Browne, also a friend of Brian's.[16] But more than anything else, perhaps, the first baby was undoubtedly the result of Brian needing loving cuddles and kind words. He also needed to brag and prove himself, while he was suffering under his controlling father, and unlike his peers, could not do what he wanted. As usual, all hell broke loose for 'what Brian had done', which was for her and him to have sex. The child was given away and the brief love affair gradually faded into history, except it kept the Cheltenham tongues wagging at least until Brian passed away; only then was he granted a respite. The story is obviously a sad one, and the consequences would have been very hard for the young girl. It was an utter, sad mistake, and it does not seem reasonable to blame either her or Brian for anything 'bad' or 'wrong'. It was a most unfortunate situation for everyone, Brian's and her parents included, but it was a matter of too young people getting mutually excited about love and each other. It happened then, it keeps happening now, and it will continue to happen.

Brian's second child was with a young girl called Valerie Corbett in 1959. They were both sixteen in the summer of 1958, when she fell pregnant, and obviously the child was unplanned. It seems they were both very fond of each other, and there was a relationship between them. Brian offered to marry Valerie but her parents were against it. The parents decided that the baby would be given for adoption, and Brian had no choice in the matter. Without blaming one or the other, they were two young people having sex, and that resulted in a pregnancy. It is totally unfair and unreasonable to say 'Brian got her pregnant', because she participated voluntarily. It is equally unfair and unreasonable to say that Brian abandoned the child, because he had no choice in the matter; the choices were made by her parents. She was too young perhaps, but so was Brian. Laying blame on either is futile in such matters. People make mistakes in their lives, and they themselves and those immediately around them move on, yet outsiders choose to harp on such unchangeable matters in someone else's past, to use them as character assessments of those involved. It has very much been used as a character assessment of Brian, which is factually and ethically wrong, because outsiders never know the ins and outs of other people's affairs, which are none of their business in the first place. Such character assessment, amounting to a character assassination, has not happened with Valerie or her parents, which is excellent as such. But it does prove the discrepancy in the minds of judgemental people and their willingness to judge against Brian but not others. Oh, how bad that Brian Jones was!

Brian's third child was also born in Cheltenham, and the baby was a result of a one-night-stand in August 1959. The mother was married, and she and her husband decided to keep the baby girl. Brian never knew about her, yet her existence has been held against Brian. What exactly was he guilty of? Guilty of having sex with the mother? It is not even known if Brian knew she was married; perhaps he did, perhaps he did not. Either way, was Brian responsible for a married woman having sex with him? One would easily be inclined to think she had had sex before and made her choice. Other than that, it seems impossible to conclude what could possibly be the problem with Brian having sex with her. Neither did he ever abandon the baby; he did not know one existed.

An important and well-known relationship in Brian's life was with Pat Andrews, and she has given interviews since and featured in articles, books and short videos. The relationship seems to have developed after Brian's death to something it was not at the time it ended, which was in August–September 1963. It seems they did not have a home together at any point in time in Cheltenham, and it is reasonable to say that it ended for Brian when he left Cheltenham for London in 1961. He took along a young school-girl, probably much to her parents' fury, but Brian kept dating many others between December 1961 and September 1963. As unsympathetic as it may sound, Richard (Dick) Hattrell, a childhood friend of Brian's, held that Brian did not want to be with her. Instead, he wanted the high-life and girls making eyes at him while performing on stage. He wanted adulation and popularity; he was a young guy. Hattrell describes Pat as an ordinary girl with no artistic skills, and he perhaps harshly considers her someone convenient to clean, cook and provide sex for Brian.[17]

Brian did not acknowledge much of a commitment to anyone at all ever, and he kept seeing whom he liked whenever he liked. It is hard to imagine Brian having any committed relationship in the so-called apartment at 102 Edith Grove, London, where the virgin musical ideas of the Stones were produced with the guys huddling up together for warmth and fiddling guitar strings to keep their fingers from freezing in the cold winter of 1962. The crummy flat the place was, it had one bedroom, a whatever of sorts for a sitting room, a kitchen in a corner, a teeny table up against the wall, and a loo. That is all there was for Brian, Mick and Keith to share, and it is difficult to imagine any of them having a sexual relationship without the other two looking on. Which, come to think of it, would not have perturbed Brian; his mind was free in the world of music with no strings attached, and the same went for his sexual enterprises. But the thought of including a mother with a baby to join the three fellows sounds like an incredibly stupid idea all round. No wonder the arrangement was as short-lived as it was ill-conceived. Besides, and whether it was fair and right or not, it is obvious that Brian did not want what he left behind in Cheltenham. For many reasons, he was not a family man to take children to outings or joyously participate in carousel rides. He did not want that life. He wanted the music scene, social circles and enticements London had to offer. He was a young musician with accidental babies in his background, so he wanted to break free.

However, Brian was allegedly deeply affected by choosing to live without the relationships from his Cheltenham years. While the first two of his babies were given to adoption and Brian could not have any contact with them, rumour has it that he missed his third Cheltenham son so much that he walked around the streets of Chelsea, looking for a small blond child, and if he spotted one, he stopped to check if it was his son. It is a bizarre story and a rumour only, with nobody on record ever saying that Brian Jones stopped them in Chelsea to check if their child was his. Realistically, Brian was an intelligent person who knew that Cheltenham was in Gloucestershire 110 miles, or 177 kms, away from Chelsea in London, and it would take someone pretty far removed from reality to start checking out other people's children to see if one of them was his own. "Excuse me, may I have a look if your child is mine? Oh wow, it isn't! Well, it just could have been you took mine from Cheltenham." It would not have gone down well with the parents or the local police. Besides, Brian had been happily seeing other girls for months on end, so maybe he was not that deeply affected with leaving his Cheltenham relationships behind after all. Unless he was deeply relieved.

Women from Brian's life have very positive memories from their times with Brian; any bitterness seems to have been wiped away. It is very understandable that there was bitterness and hurt feelings, including financial issues at the time. It is equally understandable women were hoping for more money, with Brian and the Stones becoming increasingly popular and earning exceedingly well. But there also seems to run a peculiar undercurrent of ongoing desire felt by those who claim he did not treat them right, yet their affection for him continued as did their willingness to marry him, despite their attested disgruntlement. How can it be that any mother with a child would decide many times over that she would marry the father of the child, ignoring the fact that he does not want to marry her? How does it not sink in that a man wants someone else in his life? No problem, one is inclined to think; one wants one thing and the other wants another, so they call it off and move on in different directions. - But there is the baby.

There have been millions of women who have fallen pregnant accidentally, with the parents marrying before the baby's arrival. It is completely valid to do so still, but especially in the past, when societies were more rigid than they are today, a pregnant woman's life would have been doomed unless her beau married her. That way the future of the offspring was also secured. But along the genuine, accidental pregnancies there has always existed the old game only women can play, and that is blackmailing a man into marriage by falling pregnant. The game must be as old as cockroaches on Planet Earth. It has worked for thousands of years, and it is likely to have trapped millions of men in marriages they would not have chosen, had there not been a baby on the way. Indeed, women have known extremely well how to play the game to their benefit by 'accidentally' falling pregnant, and the man had to rescue her socially; no illusions here about women and their power, intent and wishes to manipulate. They can be masters at the game and look as innocent as a fearful virgin hesitant to have her first kiss. However, there is nothing to suggest that women in Brian's life played this old game. Yet there may well have been another game used. At least it looks like it, and there are the ingredients for it.

The other game is the victim game. Women are masters of deception in the victim game, and they all have that one last option after begging, threats and tears all have failed. Many women may genuinely feel like victims; they do feel sorry for themselves, if they cannot get what they want, and they have the burden of a baby in their hands. Of course, they could blame themselves for having repeated sex with a man without contraception, but self-blame, although a sign of a level of emotional maturity in such an instance, has the downside of not being very pleasant. In fact, it is not at all pleasant, because there is nobody to go to with requests for money, and it is not at all nice, to blame oneself; leaves such a nasty after taste in your mouth. You do not want the culprit inside your own skin, where it would get crowded with the victim in residence already.

Another very reasonable alternative would be to accept half the responsibility, but it is easy to talk oneself out of it with the excuse that it is downright impossible to say which half one would be responsible for. Even then, it would be reasonable to conclude it is a joint responsibility, which means that both Mama and Papa are equally responsible for every facet of the problematic situation. But there are still unpleasant aspects in the set-up, and it just may be more financially lucrative to go and shake the proverbial apple tree to see, how many apples fall down; nothing ventured, nothing gained, and why settle for a few if you might get a whole basketful? For this method of manipulation and self-victimization the mama-to-be uses the trick of emotional projection and projects all of her own mistakes and fallacies in the situation onto the papa-to-be, and then finds fault with him for the whole shebang. After all, he really should have taken precautions, because he knew that he would not fall pregnant, so she must be a victim.

Why women in the 1960s, or ever, should continue to have unprotected sex with someone, if they do not want to get pregnant? It is understandable that these things happen in the heat of the moment. But not with repeat sex with time to consider. Every time a woman has unprotected sex she risks falling pregnant. Every woman is responsible for the choices she makes for her body and mind, and if she does not act in her own interests in this regard, why should another person do it for her? Why should a man be responsible for the woman's choice not to protect herself in repeat sex? If a woman has regular sex for e.g. two months with the same man, and the obvious happens and she falls pregnant, how is it possible that the mama-to-be would be a victim and the papa-to-be the culprit? What nonsense. Besides, it may well turn out that papa will disappear after the child arrives, if not before, but was Mama not stupid in the first place to allow herself to get caught in the situation with not taking any protection? Matters get complicated and feelings run high, but it is an over-simplification to claim that with regular sex the woman is a victim whom the man got pregnant.

Brian was smart and could see through people, and noticed their scheming long before they were willing to admit it, if ever. He saw and claimed that other Stones and the management were scheming against himself, to exclude him. Which they would deny, and blame Brian for paranoia instead. But Brian saw it, he sensed it; he had twenty years of experience in the manipulative tactics of dysfunctional people from his own home. To an outsider, the Stones internal politics including their management issues seem to have been just another arena of dysfunctional people playing their games. Equally, Brian saw it on women and in their behaviour. He had fought unfair control and manipulation ever since he was weaned off his mother's breast. He did not want to get into another controlling web in which someone would be ordering him around and spend her days finding fault with him. He loathed emotional blackmail and he loathed being run down by someone close to him. He was emotionally up in arms against being forced to marriage, because the dysfunctional one of his parents he had witnessed through his formative years, his teens and early adulthood, was nothing he wanted any part of.

One can only speculate whether any woman with Brian's baby ever played the victim card in an attempt to make Brian marry her; we can never know what is going on in someone else's mind. But a child would be a good excuse for any woman to keep hanging around or keep in contact with the father. And like any other father, Brian would have been aware that looking after a child requires money for the baby.

Brian apparently made arrangements at least for Pat to get money for their child from the Stones office. It appears she visited the office several times, to request for Brian's private address, which was denied every time. It is impossible to know what was said, and it does not matter much either, but it is reasonable to think that the office acted on Brian's advice regarding his private address, because he would want to decide who was going to front up on his door step.[18] Another way would have been to attend after a concert to ask Brian for money, but there is nothing to suggest it ever happened. Or one could have left a note in the office for Brian, to tell him no money was coming from the office staff, instead of just asking for his address. Or was it Brian's address that mattered more than anything else?

It is reasonable to think that Brian thought his advice was received and understood, so there was going to be money coming from the Stones office. It is unlikely he was aware what the office staff said, because there is nothing to suggest otherwise. In the end, it was the office of the Stones manager and under his authority. The concern now arises if Oldham and Easton were perhaps intentionally creating further problems for Brian, but we will never know either way. Consequently, what the office staff did or said is the decisive factor, and impossible to establish at this stage. But on the healthy assumption that managers are responsible for their offices, Brian was not responsible for what the office staff did.

In all fairness, Brian did contribute to all three during the time they were with Brian in London, and apparently Brian made arrangements to continue payments after August 1963. Yet Brian got blamed, and continues to get blamed, for not contributing towards their son. Obviously, getting Brian's private address was not the only way of getting money from Brian, and he had every right to keep his private address from anybody he did not want to have it. Turn it the other way round: Brian gave his private address to all those he wanted to have it, and he did not want others to front up on his doorstep uninvited. People do have a right to walk away from relationships that belong to their past with no future. People not only have a right to move on but they must do it. What did Brian supposedly do wrong in the matter?

Linda Lawrence was an important and well-known relationship in Brian's life, widely talked about in books and online. She is the mother of one his sons, and she later married Donovan. She has remained a classy lady for decades, with an apparent fond heart for Brian, which she talked about in the BBC2 documentary aired on 15 May 2023. Apparently Brian met her at the Ricky Tick club in Windsor in December 1962. She was young, fresh as a daisy, lovely all over and her parents loved her dearly. The two met and she fell in love with him, he in love with her and her parents in love with him. So when he moved in with her parents some months later, everybody in the house was in love. The days and months smoothly flowed by in grand happiness, like swans gliding across a blue summer sky, and the house residents were enjoying the pleasant warmth radiating from the sun of love. The parents were apparently very impressed with Brian, especially his pleasant manner and fame. Brian was over the moon about belonging to a loving family for the first time in his life. A late summer punch with apricots, gooseberries and blackberries with mint leaves and a good dash of Limoncello would add to the household's joy, while the first apple pie of the autumn season found an everlasting home in their loving memories of the time; a thing of beauty is a joy forever.

Then the obvious happened: Brigid, the Exalted One, Celtic goddess of birth and in charge of such matters in the locality of southern England, arranged for her mighty angels in pastel togas to herald the arrival of a baby. How could it come as a surprise to anyone? It was totally stupid of Brian to get into a pregnancy and baby mess yet again. He should have learnt by now, where to park his car.

But did young people not know in the 1960s how babies come about? Did mothers not tell their daughters what to be mindful of? It is fair to say that every mother has the responsibility to tell their daughters how to protect themselves against unwanted pregnancy. Always had, and always will have. It is a basic concern a mother has for her daughter, because a mother knows of the enormous impact a baby has on a woman's life. How could it be that two lovebirds sharing a bedroom would not be likely to result in a pregnancy? Or do parents welcoming such an arrangement have a plan that he marry her when the inevitable happens? But it was as early as in 1570, when Thomas Howell advised '*Counte not thy Chickens that vnhatched be*', so if not the lovebirds, then the parents of the lovebirds, would have been fully aware to be safe than sorry, and they cannot have been ignorant of the fact that a woman having sex with a man in most cases results in a pregnancy. Not surprisingly, Brian was not at all keen on yet another new role others had planned for him. He had over twenty years of experience with others making plans for him, and he was not going to have any of it. He moved out some 6 months later, and in the end would not marry, which he was always going to do anyway. It may be he still loved her, but the parents did not love him anymore.

And perhaps it was the 1960s values that make things look peculiar from a current point of view. Matters would be different now, but apparently the issue in the 1960s was not that a young man would be seeing an under-age young woman and having sex with her, as a consequence of which she fell pregnant. The issue was that it did not end in wedding bells, as it was expected to. As long as the bells were chiming for a couple to be joined in a so-called holy matrimony on a sunny morning, anything was fine; the goal was set before anything major happened. These days e.g. sex with an under-age person is an absolute forbidden, whereas in the 1960s the end result apparently had the power to glorify or dishonour what happened prior.

It is most amazing that any parents in the 1960s would take no notice of themselves failing their parental responsibility to protect their under-age daughter from sex and unwanted pregnancy, which would be the current take on the matter. If this was the way English society operated in the 1960s, then Brian very much fell victim to convention and narrow-mindedness, because the same conduct by all parties would these days result in a different outcome. It definitely seems that while there may not have been an actual plan to tie a young man down to a marriage, there was an awareness of the likelihood of a pregnancy, and that was not perceived as a bad thing to happen. In other words, the risk taken was a positive one.

And so it came to pass once more that Brian became the one and only person responsible for the undesired outcome, which, objectively, was the result of false expectations, unspoken intents and unmet hopes of all those involved. Yet somebody had to take responsibility for the consequences of what had transpired, and nobody else willing to share in any, Brian became the scapegoat for everyone's miscalculations by a majority vote. It is worth repeating that the issue was not what had happened and who did what, but that he would not marry. Not to forget that the marriage modelled to Brian at home was not anything he would want to have, and he did not know how to have a long- term relationship that would not suffocate him. A duck out of water was more comfortable than Brian trying on a role of a husband or father.

But who would want a marriage in which your parents-in-law love you on their terms, or else there is the door? Brian chose like any other man would. Brian had already learnt that when people did not get from him what they wanted, their love and concern for him ceased to exist. He learnt it from his own parents who wanted him to do what they wanted, and when he refused, their love was withdrawn. It makes perfect sense that Brian refused to marry. Brian knew nothing about how a loving and nurturing father behaves, and his model from back home in Cheltenham was nothing Brian wanted to repeat. Apparently Brian agreed to a settlement of £ 1,000, so it is crystal clear that he contributed. That was meant to be a settlement, which in legal terms means the matter was over and done with. However, after his death claims arose that the agreed amount was not enough and more was sought.

Anita Pallenberg was the femme fatale for Brian, although he did not want to marry her either; apparently neither of them wanted to marry. The first time they met was either in Hamburg or Munich in September 1965, and the disastrous affair continued until March 1967. In a magazine interview in February 1966, Brian said that they were both very fond of each other,[19] and in another magazine he rejected the thought of marrying any time soon, saying that marriage is a permanent thing that will soon become an anachronism, if it was not one already.[20] The two did not marry in 1966, and in March 1967 Brian was dealt with a deadly blow by the Stones entourage in Morocco. They killed his spirit and mind, and might as well have killed him physically, too. Pallenberg was not the marrying kind, and her take on Stones marriages and who should marry was that Mick and Keith should face each other eventually and they should get married before Mayor Koch, who was the Mayor of New York City between 1978 and 1989.[21]

It is bad enough to lose your leading position to your work mates in any place of work. It would rock the boat for anyone even with a balanced and positive outlook on life, but Brian had emotional scars from the past two decades, which was known to his work mates. Anyone else in Brian's position would have gone and found another place of work. But where could Brian go? It was his shop in the first place, and the shop was totally unique. He could not find another place of work similar to the one he was having, so he was stuck in a situation nobody would want to be in. On top of that, he also lost his woman to his work mate at the same time, and the combination threw him to an unimaginable nightmare with no end in sight. Except this one was not a nightmare he could shrug off in the morning, but one he had to face daily. Not only was his heart broken, but his privacy was violated severely in a way everybody would find objectionable. Nobody wants your work mate or friend to know about those private experiences you shared with someone you loved and had an intimate, sexual relationship with before. Every private moment between you and that someone else is strictly private; every detail of intimacy you shared is extremely private, and all of it is purely territorial. If you want someone new in your life, go and find one. But do not 'find' your mate's lover, and do not dump your lover and turn into a lover of his mate. It is simply evil to do so, and only a callous and unscrupulous person would do that. Words fail to describe the emotional pain inflicted on Brian. How can people be that mean and nasty, and continue to sleep well at night?

Suki Potier (1947–1981) was another important lady in Brian's life. Brian started a relationship with Suki, whose actual name was Melanie Susan Potier, in July 1967. She was a girlfriend of Tara Browne's, an Irish-born heir to the Guinness fortune, who had chosen to live in trendy London, where he was married with two sons. The marriage was not flourishing and his wife, who passed away in 2012, had become estranged, while Tara, having the financial luxury to do so, continued as a busy London socialite in the company of pretty girls, one of them being Suki. She was a passenger in the car Tara was driving on 17 December 1966, and he crashed the car into a parked truck in South Kensington, London. He died in hospital the following day, aged only 21, but Suki, aged 19, did not sustain injuries.

Brian, on the other hand, was friends with Tara Browne already and often visited his family before the accident. Brian was more than licking his wounds after the tragic first few months of 1967, which left him permanently damaged emotionally, but a new relationship seemed a comforting way forward. Suki was having her own emotional scars from the crash in December, and Brian and her were a good match for wounded doves looking for loving company. It is easy to understand that they found mutual consolation in each other's arms. It seems that Suki and Brian had a good relationship, although the intense attraction, or perhaps it was love, may have been more on her side than his.

It came to an end of sorts with Brian breaking it up around April 1969, at which time he was continuing to see doctors both for his mental and physical problems. It is possible the break-up happened because Suki wanted to marry and Brian did not, but it could also be that Suki was urging and reminding Brian to do the right thing by his health and stop drugs, alcohol and smoking completely, the necessity of which Brian would have been aware of himself. But, at the time, he was also becoming an increasingly frequent visitor to London clubs like the *Speakeasy* and the *Revolution*, where he was bound to drink, smoke and take drugs, such a combination in merry company being hard to resist. Perhaps too much so, which would have been hard for Brian to cope with. He had a bright mind, but all his life he was tormented with feelings of failure and self-loathing, and breaking up with Suki comes across as a form of self-defence, because it silenced the messenger talking about the problem: when you are distressed out of your mind about something, it is painful to hear someone talk about it. But if that someone is no longer present, you will feel better, elusive only as the relief will be. However, Suki continued to be present at Cotchford at least until early June, when she broke up with Brian because of frequent drinking bouts and rows. She probably continued to hope for a reconciliation between Brian and herself, because it appears she was very much in love with Brian. Whether she was or not, she was Brian's last lover.

Apparently she visited Cotchford with some of her female friends on 2 July, too, to pick up the rest of her belongings, but left before Brian was killed. Suki, who passed away in 1981, probably never learnt that Brian did not drown while having a swim, because it seems that Keylock and Klein entered Cotchford after she and her friends had left. For years on end there were only the fabricated witness statements, and Keylock only admitted his presence in 2009.

A dancer called Anna Wohlin from the London club the *Speakeasy* moved her things in at Cotchford around mid-June1969; Fitzgerald says Brian called him on 17 June, so it seems she moved in between 12 and 17 June.[22]. She appears to have been only a convenience to Brian, but Brian wanted her to stay for the time being, if only to annoy Keylock. Keylock objected to her presence at Cotchford probably because she was just another complication in the preparations for Brian being killed on 2 July, planned as Brian's involuntary passing seems to have been. Not that it was ever for Keylock to decide who would be staying in Brian's house anyway. But Brian had years of experience with others ordering him around on their presumed grounds of authority, and he equally had years of experience with doing exactly the opposite, so Wohlin stayed.

When Brian passed away in July 1969, matters regarding the women he would not marry and his children re-emerged from the past. There is no way Brian could have known either would happen; he thought one was getting money from the Stones office and another one had a settlement with him. However, an article in *The Mirror* in 1969 has mothers of Brian's children seeking to claim from Brian's estate, which was not possible on 2 July 1969.[23] Matters were distorted to benefit the claims, but it seems the claims were an attempt to get the impossible, meaning the settlement in a Brian paternity matter could not be wiped off the table, as it were, and there is nothing to suggest there was an arrangement for the payments from the Stones office to end on Brian's passing away. Obviously, with a settlement that is what there will be, and anyone making an unsatisfactory settlement has only himself to blame. How would it be fair to go for more, when there is a settlement in place? Also, Brian died without leaving a will, and under the law his estate passed onto his parents. *Family Reform Act 1969,* which took effect on 25 July 1969, allowed children of unmarried parents to inherit from a parent who died intestate, but that did not affect Brian's children. Brian could not know he was going to be killed and very soon as well.

It is reasonable to say that what the mothers had was insufficient for each child's lifetime. But as discussed earlier, the concept of Brian always being the only guilty party more than raises eyebrows. Although a convenient way of looking at things, it most certainly was not fair or objective. Every young woman was responsible for her part of the relationship with Brian, including the consequences thereof.

There was another baby born in 1965, and he was given away for adoption. Apparently the Stones paid the mother seven hundred pounds, and the money was later deducted from Brian's account. In return, she was supposed to remain silent about the matter. As difficult as it must be for a woman to give her baby away for adoption, there were no grounds to assume at the time that she would have further costs regarding the child, because the baby was part of the adoptive family. Also, years after Brian's passing in July 1969, the mother wrote a book and told it all, despite promising before that she would not, which was mentioned in the terms of the payment she received. Was that fair?

Nobody is trying to say Brian did all he could, but most of us only donate or willingly part with as little as possible. Most children born out of wedlock in the England of the early 1960s

(75% of them) never ever got anything from their father, whose name they may even not have known.

The above was the state of affairs on 2 July 1969, when Brian passed away, apparently murdered. He obviously did not know it was going to happen, and had made no arrangements to ease the way for those he left behind. There is no way of knowing what may have happened between Brian and his children, had he lived longer, and he could not possibly make provisions for circumstances unknown to him. Looking objectively at what was in place at the time, there was the settlement between one mother and him, the arrangement for another to get money from the office, and the third mother no longer had the child. Yes, people do change their plans, but any complaints that he should have paid more in case he was going to die are absurd; it does not happen in relationship break-ups. There may have been life insurance options available for an unforeseen death of either parent, as there are now, but Brian's children were born out of wedlock and did therefore not have any official status at the time. Not because of Brian, but because of the English system at the time.

Again, Brian became the bad, bad person who went and dropped dead, which was ill-timed for others and created further problems for them. How selfish and thoughtless of him not to do it at a more convenient time! On grounds unknown, women he had not trusted enough to marry, went against what they had said before and wanted what was not agreed. He said himself that women schemed against him, even when they said they loved him. It sounds like an odd statement from a man who has had many women, but put in the context of Brian's life it sounds perfectly logical. And was he wrong? When the relationships began, they began as stories of affection between a man and a woman, or too young women, rather. But they then became stories of more gain for the women, when the women realized who he was and became. Instead of a relationship with a man called Brian Jones, they apparently went for the man who was the Rolling Stones founder and a group member, in the same way as Diana Spencer wanted to marry a man called Charles Windsor, not because the Charlie he was as a person, but because he was the Prince of Wales and a member of the Royal Family.

Confusions also seem to arise regarding who was number one of the women in Brian's life. These concerns are of a later date than 2 July 1969, so there does not seem to have been an interest for anyone to be the irreplaceable number one in the 1960s. The books by Laura Jackson (published in 1992), Bill Wyman (published in 1997) and Terry Rawlings (published in 2014) reveal accounts regarding some life experiences with Brian being enhanced with incredible details that contradict the previous versions of the same event by the same speaker. It is astounding. The concern for an outsider interested in Brian Jones history is that some alleged events of the first-hand witnesses are unreliable, and it is an unfortunate situation. Whatever any woman from Brian's life wants to maintain, Brian was not a father drooling over his children, which also does not mean he was hostile to them. He simply was not a father who would break down in tears and be upset with the gorgeousness of his son, whom he was allegedly bouncing on his knee. Brian was not a loving, nurturing, balanced father, and he did not have a particularly good relationship with any mother after a baby was on the way, or after the birth. There is nothing to suggest that Brian favoured one child over the others. Such stories sound like make-believe to create memories of events that never existed.

Suffice to say on grounds of the information available he loved the best the woman he did not have a child with, and that is Anita Pallenberg. She was the seductress Brian fell for head over heels. Whether it was love or a co-dependency he could not shake off, his feelings for her were hotter and more passionate than for any other woman he knew. While it was a destructive relationship for Brian, he was keenly and intensely involved. Stories about lasting bonds Brian allegedly had are pure fiction, because there is not a bond he did not break with any woman in his life, except the one he had with Anita. Brian was never loyal to any woman he was involved with, and he did not remain longing for anyone but her. But he was not and is not responsible for people's fantasies and dreams; millions of people have their own.

In all probability, Brian fathered more children than anyone knows of. All of that happened many decades ago, and fortunately most women have moved on, including those who probably had his child but we know nothing of. It is essential in general that people move on from anything in their past. Any woman from Brian's life, or from some other famous man's life, who did not move on when the relationship ended, would certainly have issues with what was, what is and what will be, commonly known as reality. It could equally happen to a man, perhaps, although men do think in different ways, be it to their benefit or their detriment. But what would happen to a woman who fails to move on from a relationship with a famous man, be he dead or alive?

She would never become a person in her own right, and her life would continue filtered through a kaleidoscope of distorted images. If she did not find a point from which to start afresh, the thoughts of what she desired and hoped for in the past would become her identity; she would become to be known as one who knew the man she could not have, and her identity would revolve around that in the eyes of others. Time would stop, and she would not become anything else. Her twisted will to get what was not available would become the focal point on which her life is built.

If she fails to move on, the distorted image of him as her husband or the love story of the millennium, neither of which ever existed, impregnates her brain matter so that the only thoughts produced emerge like crocus buds in spring, ready to burst to new life. But woe is me; when they do open, inside them is the illusion of a relationship that never was, and the bud cannot produce a blossom because there is no life inside. Year after year, the same illusion in the flower bed of her mind that refuses to accept reality, keeps producing more sordid bulbs of her failed desires, so more and more detail gets woven into the illusion from the past. The fabrication, thicker with every passing year, only remotely resembles the truth from long ago. And the woman remains blind to the fact that all she had was an illusion she kept alive with manure in the flower bed of her mind.

6
Just Another Social Bastard?

There are claims that Brian's heart had a darkness that urged him to explore blues music which, allegedly, was devil's music. Devil's music for one because his mother said so while smashing his guitar, for which reason she can hardly be regarded as an objective or reliable source of information, be it on devil or blues music, but mainly because the concept of devil's music comes from the story of a young man called Robert Johnson (1911–1938) in Mississippi of the American south. His short life of 27 years is as poorly documented as is his death, but what is known is that he was an itinerant musician wandering from town to town and playing his music on street corners. His fond interest in ladies and popularity among them did nothing to attract positive attention from his fellow men, but he became highly regarded for his musical talent in his favoured style of music, and women liked his smooth manner and keenness for feminine attraction. But a great musician he was, and as would typically happen in a case of a person of achievement in surrounds of a limited number of people with reading and writing skills, the lack of facts and a source of information to fall back on gave rise to many folk tales. The one most closely associated with Robert

Johnson is that he sold his soul to the devil in exchange for being able to play the best bluesy music. It is a folk tale and not a historical fact.

A similar story is told by Johann Wolfgang von Goethe, a German playwright, poet and novelist (1749–1832), in his drama *Faust*, which, in turn, goes back to an alchemist and magician man called Johann Georg Faust, who possibly lived ca. 1470–1560 in Germany of the Holy Roman Empire at the time. He was an itinerant, and consequently tales and stories about him began to emerge in different parts of the country, resulting in Dr Faustus in folk tales. By the time Goethe lived around 300 years later, the various tales rampant in the past had become a well-known folk tale of a man who was successful but depressed in his life, and who was then approached by the devil and offered unlimited knowledge of all things imaginable for twenty-four years, after which he would render his soul to the eternal use by the devil as desired. And Faust accepted the bargain. – But what do these stories have to do with Brian Jones of Cheltenham?

Absolutely nothing as such, but because it is a convenient way to paint Brian's heart black before he was weaned off his mother's breast, the stories, which are stories only, come in handy as some sort of proof that there was something of the devil in Brian, despite the connection remaining tenuous at best. Realistically, and sprinkled with a smidgeon of common sense, such claims are as profoundly ludicrous as are stories of the Holy Ghost impregnating Mary mother of Jesus, as a consequence of which Jesus was part human and part something divine. The truth is that Brian was a human being made by a woman and a man, and Jesus was exactly the same. The ignorance of the Jesus claim goes back to the lack of knowledge at the time of a man's sperm fertilising a woman's ovum, resulting in a child that consists of the combination of the parents. It also goes back to the need of people in the first century AD wanting to create a most unusual story to emphasize how unusual and unique Jesus was for the purposes they had in mind. The method is exactly the same as is with Brian Jones; some have a need to make Brian sound particularly undesirable, and what better way than make up a story of him having some of the devil in himself. They do stop short of calling him a Rosemary's baby of sorts, but that was a film and taken as such, whereas Brian is seriously meant to have a devil of some sort in him. – If you still wish to argue about the Holy Ghost business, please consider that the term 'Holy Ghost' comes from Hebrew, in which all nouns are either masculine or feminine, and 'Ruach Hakodesh' for 'Holy Ghost' is feminine, and two females no baby ever produceth, so happen it did not. And incredible as it may sound to the ear of a Doubting Thomas, Brian's birth was the result of his parents' love life.

Brian's first Rolls Royce, a fabulous Rolls Royce Silver Cloud II (1959) had vehicle plates DD 666. It is either ignorance or ill-will maintaining for decades now that Brian was closely affiliated with all things evil, so much so that he chose DD for 'devil's disciple' and 666 for the beast of some sort he was. Complications arise straight away with the fact that Brian bought the car from George Harrison, although some say it was from John Lennon. Either way, the plates would have been on the vehicle, when Brian purchased it, because a change in vehicle registration in 1963 added a letter after the three digits. It is possible that given half a chance, Brian would have enjoyed choosing 666 for his Rolls, just to stir things up for the traditional PPP-league, PPP being short for *Pompous Pretenders of Prudence*, but there is nothing to show that the plates were ever changed.

Besides, devil did not have disciples. It was the other guy on the good side who did. But because those plates do not have a letter after the three digits, the vehicle was probably registered in the 1950s and definitely before 1963. Letters DD say that the vehicle was registered before 1965, and that must have happened in one of the county councils throughout Britain, with each county having an office keeping a record of drivers and licenses. Each local office was called *Driver and Vehicle Licensing Agency (DVLA)*. British vehicle registration was centralized in 1965, with the headquarters currently in Wales. But the letters DD on Brian's Rolls simply denoted the registration region of Deeside to Shrewsbury, with the local office in Chester. Brian could not choose the letters, and they did not mean 'devil's disciple' any better SS meant 'super sexy'; SS simply denoted the region of Scotland with the DVLA office in Glasgow.

Claims that Brian had a 'flawed' character, character 'deficiencies' and the like must go back to some perceived understanding of what a flawless character would be, or what a sufficient or abundant character is like. Logically, behind these claims lies the assumption that the person making such claims knows what the word 'character' means. However, instead of being a straight-forward matter, it is more like a cornucopia overflowing with the abundance of aspects and variants that a lay-person would not think of. But whatever 'character' may be, it is not an entity Mother Nature places inside the human body for the purpose of operating it, much in the way an engine is placed inside the body of a car to run it. It is far more complicated, and the time for its fruition takes about two decades. In comparison, to start a car, you turn the key clockwise and the engine will be purring before you have time to start picking your nose behind the wheel.

Modern personality theories think that personality consists of temperament and character, with temperament being the primary foundation of personality. Temperament is thought to be present at birth, and it is thought to cover the aspects of your personality you were born with. This inborn temperament is what you were furnished with in your biology. It is considered the beginning of your personality, and it excludes all experiences you make ever. Over months and years that follow after your birth, all experiences you make develop your character. – Examples of what temperament entails are your general energy level, emotional responsiveness, curiosity and mood. It is easy to understand that these aspects are inborn and differ between individuals, as we know from experience that some people are more energetic than others, or more curious and inquisitive than some others. Equally, it is easy to understand that these aspects will have an effect on how you grow to learn and experience life; if you are curious about matters around you, you are likely to learn more and more quickly, and being moody will have a direct effect on how you experience life in general.

Character, on the other hand, represents your moral, ethical, and social attitudes and beliefs. It is suggested that character develops as soon as you start facing environmental challenges; it is not possible to establish when exactly it begins, as experiments on such matters cannot be carried out. Such environmental challenges may be minor, requiring gradual adjustment with no strong, lasting effect, but they can also be harsh or difficult in being unforeseen and unpredictable. When that happens, and especially when it happens repeatedly, character patterns are likely to occur in adulthood. Or put in another way; if such harsh challenges occur, they more or less predict specific problems in adulthood; trauma leaves its marks. – Examples of character traits are honesty, loyalty, generosity, integrity and ambition.

Moving on to personality, which is the connection of temperament and character, although it also encompasses thought and behavioural patterns that emerge in every life situation. Your personality represents who you are as a person. It is the large umbrella under which shelter all your inherited traits, natural inclinations and beliefs that make you your unique *you*. It contains all and everything about you; all your behaviours, thoughts, beliefs, traits, experiences; it is the home for all those warts, roses and daffodils that make you the person you are. Whom you choose as a friend, what you choose to wear, what you like for art, music, fun, and how you conduct yourself with others in any given situation are aspects and reflections of your personality. It can influence major parts of life, such as work, social circles, activism, also criminality, and it may determine choices you make. It may also determine how your relationships turn out, and the outcome of your goals, be it positive or not desired.

Character can be seen as your essence, while your personality is how you express that essence. In this sense, they are inter-dependent in both directions. – Examples of personality traits are independence, neuroticism, sociability and extraversion or introversion.

Considering that the issues discussed above invariably apply to everyone, where would we place a 'flawed character' or a 'character deficiency' and their respective opposites 'flawless character' and 'sufficient or abundant character'? Does anybody know a person with such a character? We already discussed that character develops as reactions to environmental challenges, which, understandably, are different for every individual. If they are different for everyone, we cannot establish an objective and definable level of sufficiency. And if we cannot define a 'sufficient' character, it follows that we cannot define 'insufficient' or 'flawed' either; for that to occur, we would need a neutral point zero of 'sufficiency' from which an acceptable degree of variation can be determined. There also remains the mine field of miscellaneous concerns how one could assess a theoretical 'sufficiency', when for a clear classification all backgrounds would have to be alike, yet they never are for individuals.

But having a look at the character traits honesty, loyalty, generosity, integrity and ambition, mentioned earlier, you can compare any group of people you know, and you do not need to know them privately or intimately to make observations. You will soon find out that not only is everyone an individual with different character traits, but the same character traits appear in different degrees and in different contexts. Your comparison will never be a scientific presentation of those characteristics in different people, because you can only ever offer an opinion and perception of what you are observing. Thinking of honesty: everybody's honesty depends on the situation and interests of the person in question, and it is impossible to vouch for anyone's honesty ever. Loyalty is a characteristic people apply to different people, and they can also be loyal to a cause they want to promote. People can be generous at different times in their lives, depending on their ability and circumstances to display it. Integrity is something we expect of everyone and hardly ever get. So whatever you think you may be observing maybe be an illusion only.

The essence of the exercise is that among those you observed, you cannot point out anyone who would excel more than the others, or fare worse than the rest. Everyone can always do better in a number of ways. Equally, everyone can always perform below his standard level either accidentally or intentionally. What is certain is that nobody would reach a level of character sufficiency, if such a concept existed, and nobody would fall below it either. So why is it that Brian Jones continues to be the exception in the history of mankind to be singled out and judged as 'flawed' of 'deficient in character'? What authority does anyone have to make such a claim?

A matter worth consideration is a normal personality in terms of psychology, and while that does not mean that any person falls under a definition of a normal person in general, the definition of a normal or abnormal personality in terms of psychology is a different matter. A normal person in that regard can be considered a person with no mental illness, and an abnormal person can be considered a person with a mental disability or illness. Abnormal behaviour means actions that are unexpected and often evaluated negatively because they differ from typical or usual behaviour. A person behaving in a way that as such differs from the expectations of standard norms in the society where the behaviour occurs is not mentally ill, and neither does reckless or irresponsible behaviour equal a mental illness. But not all unexpected actions are abnormal only because they differ from typical or usual behaviour; people are tempted to label others with conduct that they perceive to be reckless or irresponsible as abnormal behaviour, to give an example, but people applying such labels are only expressing their disapproval and lack of boundaries that differ from those of their own.

Normality involves an ability to adapt or adjust to changes in life or in the environment, and abnormalities are issues that prevent an individual from coping with these changes, or behaviour that results in failures to adjust adequately or appropriately to the environment or situation, amounting to maladaptation and maladjustment. Normality includes an ability not to distort any experiences; an ability to change through experiences made; as well as an ability not to resort to defensiveness in the face of criticism. An important factor in psychological normality is emotional stability, which means an ability to feel calm and manage emotions, and feeling positive about oneself and one's life and future.

Brian was in psychiatric care in 1967 and remained so until his passing. It is not known what he was receiving help for, so there is no information to base any allegations of a mental illness in him. The information he shared with medical specialists or staff at Priory Clinic remains private, as it should. Seeking psychiatric help does not indicate a mental illness as such. All it means is that the person sought help with a medical professional in that field. However, it seems that Brian thought he had a mental problem yet he lacked an understanding of it, possibly as a result of the appalling and abysmal treatment he received from his parents; he had well and truly internalized claims that he was a bad person with problems and his ways needed to be mended. Consequently, he apparently concluded he was having schizophrenia. This comes up in Fitzgerald's book, with Brian handing over to Nicholas a book he had read and was impressed with. It was *George Arbuthnott Jarrett* by Bernard Toms, a Welsh novelist, and the book was a recent arrival in the book world at the time, having been published in January 1965.

The book is an introspective analysis of the main character with perhaps schizophrenic tendencies or a split personality, although we are talking about a fictitious character in a novel and not a real person. The George part of the character is similar to a Rolling Stone from the 1960s: a feisty rebel against all strictures of convention, appalled at the rules the polite establishment was enforcing on how to behave and what to do. Arbuthnott, the other character in Toms' book, was George's mate, his conservative conscience and defender of morality and adjustment.

Considering that everyone has different aspects for their personality, it is difficult to see any mental disease in the matter as such, but it was predictable that the book would strike a chord with everyone with the ability to evaluate matters from different angles. However, and importantly, Brian very much related to the character in the book. He was an avid reader of literature and perhaps found an explanation for the many problems he was going through in Bernard Toms' book, as well as a validation of not being completely out of his mind. He had a keen interest in matters supernatural, also reading in the Bible, trying to work out what it was all about, and he was interested in matters of the mind. He knew he was not coping.

In a clipping from a publication, and it may be from a newspaper or a magazine, Brian talks about mental illness. The year and name of the publication are close to impossible to establish, although on the basis of his hair length and the black-and-white stripy top, it is likely to be from 1964 or 1965, and on the basis of the font in printing, it is likely to be from *Melody Maker* magazine, with the last issue of the publication out in December 2000:

BRIAN JONES'S [sic] *BRAVE NEW WORLD:*

"My world would be a world without sickness...a world where sickness of the body and of the mind cease to exist. I'd like lots of money spent on neuro-research, to find out what causes mental illness. When man can understand the human brain he'll understand everything. A world without sickness would be a world without cruelty, and that's everything."[24]

As discussed, Brian's character cannot be concluded to be any more 'flawed' or to have character 'deficiencies' any more than any other person could have; character cannot be flawed or deficient. Such claims, on the one hand, show that those making such comments do not know what they are talking about. On the other hand, they raise questions about the motivation of the person making such comments about another person. Perhaps it is a disapproval of something they think Brian did, perhaps it is merely a wish to find fault with Brian; make him look bad to make the others look better. Or perhaps they simply did not like Brian Jones ever. Be it any of those, or something else, people making such comments have an agenda of their own, and those comments say nothing about Brian. How could they, being ludicrous? But they do say something about those making such comments; beauty, or lack thereof, is in the eye of the beholder.

And at this crossroads, which quickly turns into a busy roundabout, we run into popular arguments about Brian:

1. He was nothing but a trouble maker.
2. There was some of the devil in him.
3. Speak well of him and you are judged a stupid person with an obsession.
4. Speak ill of him and you are judged an intelligent person with a balanced mind.
5. He was a misunderstood person with a tragic life.
6. He was a misunderstood hero.

The first four are easy to dismiss as nonsense. They are either comments reflecting lack of knowledge and mental maturity, or pure ill intent, on behalf of the speaker. They are gibberish with no objective validity, all propelled by a dark motivation, whatever it may be. With those four ruled out there are two remaining. It seems hard to argue he was a hero, because social bravery was nothing he was involved with, nor did he ever seek to be so. He was a hero in his own life, but most of us are, although not everyone. But what he most certainly was is a person with a tragic life, and he was most certainly misunderstood. He was severely misunderstood by most around him. Some seem to have had an understanding for him in some respects; Linda and her mother come across as people who had some understanding of Brian's personality. But most by far did not understand him at all, mainly because they did not want to bother, it being easier to find fault with him. And the most important of those who did not understand him at all were perhaps the other Stones, Andrew Oldham and Anita Pallenberg. The public or press did not have much of an understanding of Brian's personality, and how could they, but the public had a strong appreciation of Brian as the musician and person they perceived him to be, and he was adored for his music, good looks and dress style.

The way his tragic life unfolded was not because he was misunderstood. In Brian's Rolling Stones years people could not know much about his privacy in general, and even less about his past in Cheltenham. Also, those who were close to Brian and therefore probably knew details of Brian's bad Cheltenham years were in no way responsible for any of what happened back then. But please do not hasten to think they were innocent bystanders in the destruction of Brian Jones.

It makes no difference whatsoever what you think or how you regard the person you know is in need of help; you are free to love him to bits or consider him the lowest scum ever born. The issue is not the other person. The issue is you and that you will always be responsible for your own conduct at all times. There is no justification for thinking you are free to do what you like and you are not responsible for the pain it causes to another person. In terms of setting individual psychological boundaries, we must take responsibility for how we feel, and sorting out one's feelings is the responsibility of the individual. Indeed, we may face a situation ostensibly too overwhelming to cope with, yet we know we must soldier through it, to continue living.

But the buck does not stop there. If you intentionally inflict unreasonable emotional pain on someone, you are responsible for it, on top of which you will be aware that you are already failing ethics abysmally. While unreasonable emotional pain may be challenging to define beyond an individual level of tolerance, it most certainly includes the destruction of another human being's personality, which happened with Brian. If you see that a person cannot cope emotionally with the results that your conduct towards him has caused, you must show sympathy and support to him, and offer help. Like it or not, you are responsible for getting help for him. It is malicious, evil conduct to rub salt in his wounds and then complain he deserved it because he was no good to start off with. It is inexcusable and low below the lowest, and something only humans do. Animals do not, including cockroaches.

As said before, those around Brian during his years in London were not responsible for the damage inflicted by his family in Cheltenham. But after he moved to London, everyone around him was responsible for the way they treated him. If they treated him well, they deserve to be thanked and applauded. If they treated him badly, they deserve to be scolded and reprimanded. There never was any need for them to understand Brian and his past. People are not expected to know other people's past, nor would it be reasonable to do so. But it does not matter in any which way whether they do or not, because if they treat other people with decency, respect and kindness, the old wounds do not come to the surface to be exacerbated by new mistreatment. All Brian needed for people around him to do was to treat him the way another mere mortal deserves to be treated. Those still around, who continue to maintain he was horrible to deal with, cannot use it as an excuse to have mistreated him then, or mistreating him verbally now. Do not mistreat another living creature, because you are responsible for what you do!

The standard excuse in cases of domestic violence is that he beat her up, because the sheer frustration he was experiencing over her complaints made him explode. That is most certainly not true; what makes a person explode, if that be the term, is his inability to deal with his own feelings and actions under pressure. You cannot blame the victim for your conduct, regardless of how you felt or what you were thinking at the time, and regardless of how you regard the person. Do not mistreat another living creature!

Those around Brian used him, abused him and schemed against him, and the way he was treated was deplorable and substandard. He was mistreated left, right and centre. Brian was destroyed because those in his life did not treat him in the way a decent person would treat another person; there was not an ounce of kindness or appreciation in the way he was kicked around and used as a doormat for years. He was destroyed because of other people's egotistical desires, weak male egos, greed, callousness and nastiness, and not because of his own weaknesses. His demise was not that he was misunderstood, but that he was betrayed and abandoned by others by 1968, and agonized Brian disintegrated into the unchartered depths of his enmeshed existence. He was a mentally and physically damaged man who did not understand how to live, and who sought love in the wrong places and in wrong ways. He was a gifted, creative musician and more sexually and visually attractive than the rest of the Stones put together with icing sugar sprinkled on top. None of the other Stones was even remotely as attractive as Brian, and they undoubtedly envied him for a number of reasons. Which, of course, they would deny.

Brian Jones did not destroy himself any better than an abandoned dog does. Like an abandoned dog, he was destroyed by mistreatment and lack of love from human beings around him.

7
Brian the Artist

Brian was a highly gifted and creative person. Again, it does not matter whether you like or dislike his skill and creative contributions, perhaps because you do not like him as the person you perceive him to have been. Any personal opinion of Brian does not affect his personality or artistic creativity, and an emotionally intelligent, non-vindictive person without ill intent easily distinguishes between one and the other. Everyone is responsible for the application of openness in their thinking, but you can always choose to remain thick as well.

There are many ways of describing the system that encases life as we see it, and just as many ways of categorizing issues around the matter. For the purposes of describing the visions of the Rolling Stones founder Brian Jones, it is good to focus on the basic categories of form and content, because life, as the experience we have, manifests itself on these two important levels. They are the keys into an artistic vision. Which, for its part, was very much what inspired Brian's strong fondness for Blues music and his ardent desire to make music.

Form is what we see, feel and do, and that means the everyday life that we run and our human conduct, including any actions it involves. It is deeply influenced by rules and traditions of our culture, thereby varying to some extent from culture to culture. But it is always the direct involvement of our body and its automatic sensory system with anything outside our body, which itself is within the society we are part of but have no direct control over. It includes all our individual customs and habits, as well our religious affinities or belief systems, because they arise in our bodies and directly affect our body on an individual basis only; there is no external, discernible source available that would cause the same conduct in different individuals or different groups of individuals. It may be that individuals share the same religion, but their inner, private perception and understanding of it is unique to the individual.

Examples for this are how we learn how to greet and respond to a greeting, or to silence down and keep our body passive with no sudden movements, when we want to become a member of the party we want to blend in. Or how to go about feelings such as greed, hunger, avarice or anger. Or learn the borders of acceptable behaviour, or when and where to step in, when we see a problematic situation we think may need intervention. Or what we are to think during a religious service, or how we are supposed to see the religious beliefs, practices and traditions in our society, if we wish to participate in the religious functions we choose. Or what to teach our children for them to blend in more easily with their class mates. Essentially, everything about life and interaction between people is a matter of learning how to do it, so we call it the form. And life may remain on the mere functional level of form for many, if not for most; a lot depends on your aptitude, ways of thinking and choices made.

Content is the level where individual meaning is put into our actions, ways of thinking and perceptions that are on the form level. E.g. loyalty is a concept that affects our conscious behaviour, but the depth or lack thereof is the content we give to the concept, and whether we involve other aspects in our content of loyalty; we can feel a different kind of loyalty to different people, and the borders of loyalty may differ for different people we want to be loyal to. E.g. maternal love is an absolute loyalty a mother usually feels for her child, but it is unlike any other loyalty she feels for others, yet her acts are still consistent with the conduct of a person loyal to another. Music is a form we all experience with our ears, but how we hear it, i.e. what we perceive it contains, is vastly different between individuals. Equally, literature is something we all know of, but its meaning and content can vary to no end, way beyond words, and music has a way of expressing feelings way beyond language. Alternatively, it can be a mere temporary, pleasant listening exercise of something of your choice.

Content also entails what some see beyond what an average person sees and feels, because people have different skills and capabilities. That is the world that artists see, and it is that vision, that content, which is highly individual and only comes from within, as eloquently expressed by Samuel Taylor Coleridge (1772–1834), an English poet and philosopher:

"I may not hope from outward forms to win.
The passion and the love whose fountains are within."

It comes from within, and it is the essence of art. Art is more than a skill or an ability; it is a passion, or call it an extension of personality if you will, that engages one's skill and ability to enhance what already is there, or to come up with something new. It is the expression of creative skill and imagination in a sensory form, be that visual or audible, or something you gain an experience of with your hands. It produces works than can be appreciated primarily for their beauty or emotional power. It is an individual way of grasping the world beyond the physical one, to enter a spiritual experience or one of enthralling beauty beyond words. Or depths of extreme horror.

That artistic passion and force does not come about in bouts, bursts or flurries. It does not look you up in sessions or at intervals, be they days or weeks apart. Or annually. Actions of humans may happen like that, and when they do, we may repeatedly manoeuvre in façades, or forms, whose meaning echoes from a force we do not know. If you are not aware of this, you will not understand beyond form, but will fall victim to the illusion that the façade is all there is. Brian knew intuitively that the façades of life and games people play hide real life. He understood the forms and levels of content that life has, and he lived in a world most people did not understand. They could not, because they knew nothing about it.

But artists are individuals of fire, and if your chemistry is one of calm control, your creative soul was not present when the Tower of Babylon was built, at which time you could have experienced not being able to understand or being understood. But if you were there, your heart and mind were touched with the fire of creation, to bring forth an understanding beyond what will always elude the inattentive human eye and ear.

Brian was a true artist of fierce passion and an attentive mind. Being an artist, he also suffered intense pain and hurt, which sharpened his senses; life is not only a dance on roses but a struggle for violets as well, and every rose bush with the most alluring fragrance has its stems covered in thorns. Brian Jones was very much a loner in his creative world that probably very few people, if anyone, shared. George Harrison was close to Brian in what they did, and it is possible Brian shared more with George than we are aware of. Brian's bright mind and good education made him outshine most by far, and he outshone every single other Stones member. When you outshine others, you become lonely and vulnerable, and Brian was lonely and vulnerable from the beginning. Group dynamics is a tricky business, and the rule of thumb is that anyone who stands out will be bitched about and bullied, which happened with Brian. It also affected his relationships with women, although women did not want to accept it; they could not match his mind, so all there remained for him to share with them was his body and sentimentality to an extent. And cleaning, cooking and ironing, interspersed with sex.

The artist in Brian could not turn latent, because it could never be satiated; the source of his gifted spirit was creation that knows no time, place or bounds. In his heart burnt the eternal fire of life, and his creative spirit flowed through his fingers onto what he touched. Born of the sun, he glowed in the gold and red palette of fire for music and love, and seduction was his method of bringing forth beauteous exultation, be it in musical instruments or women his hands made love to. He clothed his spirit from head to toe in song, and his life, like a tumultuous storm that he rode on, was the labour pains of Mother Nature giving birth to a new musical expression. Sound was what Brian was attuned to, and sound was his way of opening the doors to his creativity. Sound and song are received and experienced through ear, and the meaning of words is part of sound and music, believe or not, equally received and experienced through ear. Colour is also part of the simultaneous game.

Sound and song played an important role in sharing information thousands of years ago, and they worked much in the way writing and text is used for the same purpose these days. Information was recited and sung, which was a means of employing a way to remember history, family lines and rules of society, in the same way as religious chants still entail the essence of an individual's devotion to the particular religion. Outside religious chants, sound and song as a means of providing essential information has ceased to exist. But back in the day, when sound and song were widely used for the purpose, they replaced an individual's ability to read and write, neither of which was always available. Learning a song or a chant passed on the message from one individual to another, from a group to another, from generation to generation, through decades and centuries passing by.

It is easy to see how a recital in the form of a monologue would naturally employ sound and song, to make it easier for the performer to remember the words and for the listeners to follow the content. The addition of a rhythm and a melody flowed as if by itself, to share the recital with further ease and adding to the enjoyment of performing it and receiving it. From there runs a direct path onto a road with two-way travel between song and sound on the one side, and words on the other, both having a continuous effect on each other, like the wind blows golden, mature wheat in the field forward and backward, and the waves of the sea conform to the will of the wind.

In ancient Greek, song and poetry walked hand in hand; poetry was written words in song. Classical Greek drama had a chorus fundamentally different from a modern-day choir in the background used today. A Chorus was a group of actors describing and commenting on the action of the play, using recitation and dance, while rhythmically moving in a circle as they chanted their lines. They were part of the whole performance and presented the play to the audience as much as individual actors did. It was a powerful combination of sound, song, rhythm and dance coming together, no different from the Rolling Stones performing to an audience, with the audience becoming part of the performance through their singing and dancing on the worldly stage of all things human.

The medieval troubadours recited their poems in song, and the ballad singers in the time of Elizabeth I always sang their verses, although they were actually poems. But as before, sound, song and poetry presented themselves as a unity of different aspects of the whole. And Brian Jones sensed it. He had the ear for it. Today we receive a poem in a written form: in other words, it is the eye that takes it in, because the poem only appears as text on a page. But it is still the ear and not the eye that decides how we appreciate it, because when we read it, we hear it in our mind, and the ear is still our judge to decide yay or nay. No matter how you look at it, sound, song and words are siblings in the same family.

Poetry today no longer has the beauty it had even 150 years ago, and our sense of beauty for sound and song have been corrupted by the discord of sound in many so-called styles in music, such as rap. Rhyme is a method that aids any wordings, be they in poems or lyrics of a song, to complement the words with a melody and vice versa; we are now back to music here. Rhymes make the text flow, and they help the words echo the melodies lost. The magic will always be thought, feeling and music brought together. The best is reached, when words are made with music and not for music, glorified with the melody and special effects, if desired. Poetry and music go hand in hand, and both are hard to define and impossible to limit. They open doors beyond what words can express. Poetry is like a perfect union of music and meaning, or sound and emotion. But poetry can also go one way only, in impregnating the mind with sound and rhythm on the one hand, and intense feeling on the other. Between the extremes is a vast playground of sound, song and senses.

Sounds as words is more common than one would imagine, and an excellent example is *Jabberwocky* by Lewis Carroll. The poem was published in 1871. Seemingly senseless, it is anything but senseless, yet it is not the words as such but the sound that is everything in the poem. And the beauty of it is that the meaning and message is decided by the reader; he can make it what he wants it to be. The whole meaning of the poem is in the depth or lightness, combined with intensity, of sounds that set the pace, action and direction. All it has is sound and rhythm, and the words, meaningless as such, gain their meaning from their sound alone. The reader can read it out loud, to turn it into an astounding piece of drama:

"Twas brillig, and the slithy toves

Did gyre and gimble in the wabe;
All mimsy were the borogoves,
And the mome raths outgrabe."
"Beware the Jabberwock, my son!
The jaws that bite, the claws that catch!
Beware the Jubjub bird, and shun
The frumious Bandersnatch!"
He took his vorpal sword in hand:
Long time the manxome foe he sought —
So rested he by the Tumtum tree,
And stood awhile in thought.
And as in uffish thought he stood,
The Jabberwock, with eyes of flame,
Came whiffling through the tulgey wood,
And burbled as it came!
One, two! One, two! And through and through
The vorpal blade went snicker-snack!
He left it dead, and with its head
He went galumphing back.
"And hast thou slain the Jabberwock?
Come to my arms, my beamish boy!
O frabjous day! Callooh! Callay!"
He chortled in his joy.
"Twas brillig, and the slithy toves
Did gyre and gimble in the wabe;
All mimsy were the borogoves,
And the mome raths outgrabe."

Sounds and words can also give the reader a sense of movement not present on the page where the writing is. The examples below are from Robert Southey's poem *How the waters come down at Lodore,* and you can hear the rushing and rhythm of the rapids, and the power of the water forcing itself forward over every obstacle. Lodore is the home of the waterfalls near Keswick in The Lake District of England:

"How does the Water
Come down at Lodore?"
From its sources which well
In the tarn on the fell
From its fountains
In the mountains
Its rills and its gills…
…
Retreating and beating and meeting and sheeting,
Delaying and straying and playing and straying
Advancing and prancing and glancing and dancing,
Recoiling, turmoiling, toiling and boiling…

In essence, sound, song and words work together for a combined effect that manifests itself in the way an individual perceives a meaning beyond what any of the three can render on their own. While a musical scale is a set of musical notes ordered by fundamental frequency, the notes also express depth and height of each sound, which, in turn is represented in our speech. If speech, i.e., what we say, is in writing, we use letters of the alphabet to convey sounds. If what we say is in spoken form, we use sounds, especially vowels but also consonants with no stops, to denote height of sounds, just as we do on a musical scale. Letters of the alphabet are just letters, and they are not sounds, e.g., the letter k is a letter and it is pronounced as 'kay', but the sound it makes is the release of the blockage formed by our tongue against the upper teeth on each side towards the back of the mouth, and that sounds somewhat like 'kheh'. It is the sounds that matter here, and not the alphabet. Sounds do have an alphabet of their own, and that is produced by the International Phonetic Association, and while it is a most interesting world of its own, it is not related to the discussion here.

Thinking of 'open' vowels *a, e, o*, it is easy to see they can be used in a melody just on their own: they simply flow, because there is no stoppage in the airway in your mouth. In contrast to 'open' vowels there is also *i,* and in languages other than English there are many others, but we are talking about English here. The absence of a stoppage also applies to soft consonants, or perhaps they should better be called 'liquid' consonants, because while they are consonants, they are easy to combine with vowels without a stoppage in the air flow. They are basic music, and you can add a melody to them, to please your ear.

Brian Jones had a particularly acute sense of hearing sound and minute variations in it. It is reflected in the way he pronounced extremely well languages he did not know at all, or not particularly well. His skill to pronounce German was admirable, and he had an ear discerning enough to differentiate between consonant sounds in German and Swedish, although the difference between the two is not particularly great. Yes, it is discernible, but not particularly distinct and hard to pick up by a foreigner. The difference in the pronunciation of those sounds between German and English is greater, and the difference in pronunciation of *sh* between the two languages is clearly discernible. But Brian had an ear for it; he was a musicophile, he was an artist. Brian instinctively knew that sound, rhythm, words, music and writing go back to the same creative force of eternal flow of life.

With sound, song and the flowing effect of beautiful combinations familiar to Brian from early on, it is not surprising that he excelled in writing as well. Gordon Harper, Brian's English teacher at Dean Close Junior School in Cheltenham, said that he considered Brian outstanding in composition. Brian's previous teacher in the preparatory department shared his view, and remarked on Brian's ability as early as the age of seven.[25] It seems none of those essays from his younger years have remained, but it is also possible that his family kept them.

Also, the Stones early interviews in particular attract attention to Brian's excellent command of English vocabulary and the ease with which he uses words of Latin origin. His pronunciation was precise and upmarket; it was the voice of a person at home in the world of reading and writing in solitude. Of course, his eloquent vocabulary got up the noses of other Stones whose vocabulary was far more limited, and complaints were made that Brian used the words intentionally to mock others. Which is clearly pure rubbish, because it is not possible that others could read his mind.

Brian wanted to do more writing, and he spoke about this desire of his in an article published in *Record Mirror* magazine on 12 February 1966. He said what he needed was more support and encouragement, and if someone supported him emotionally in this regard, he would be able to do it; his problem was not that he did not know how to write, but, as always, his lack of confidence. And we know who to thank for his deep-rooted lack of self-confidence originating in lovely Cheltenham.

Sadly, in all probability we lost a writer; perhaps a poet, or an essayist, with Brian's early passing. He had the gift of sublime expression, and we are likely to have lost gentle, eloquent or vociferous verbal art woven into stanzas or sentences, like pearls onto silk thread.

The poem below was probably written by Brian, but the date is not known. It may be he wrote it with someone in mind, but it could be an imaginary person he ardently wished for. There is no way of telling whom he may have had in mind, if anyone, although claims have emerged it was about one or another girl-friend of his. Such claims remain without proof.

Thematically the poem is dark; it speaks of disillusionment and pain, for which reason it is likely to go back to times after March 1967, which was the beginning of his most painful years. He seems to have understood the song of his life, meaning the melody our lives have, unique to everyone. He speaks of lack of understanding, hopes and wishes that remain unsatisfied for him, yet he still hopes he will be able to rise above the pain he endured from small-minded people that scorned and ridiculed him. He does not want to fight windmills; instead, he is seeking shelter and soothing rest. Just rest, peace and comfort; no fear and no tears anymore.

While it is impossible to date the poem, it is nonetheless wildly acknowledged to be written by Brian. The poem is the only example of Brian's lyrics that actually made it to a CD, and that was in 1990. It was adapted to music by Carla Olson and performed on CD in 1990 by Kristianne and Robin

Williamson. While Brian's poem remains impressive, the appreciation of the musical composition is subject to acquiring the taste for it.

> As each sharp outline
> Melts and weaves
> And undulates in time
> With the compulsive
> Rhythmic insistence
> Of each pounding musical line
> The scornful dancing lady dressed
> In black at last reveals
> She really isn't there at all
> She simply isn't real
> So thank you for being there
> -My love
> At least I know that you're real
> As I speak with you of love
> -In metaphors and in code
> A need for satisfaction grows
> But they're stories still to be told
> Of experience and fantasies.
> Of vision and of fears
> But when the visions fade
> -you'll be there
> Lying in my tears
> Thank you for being there my love
> Then I know that you're real
> If the lashing tail of paranoiac fears
> Strike my smarting face
> Your understanding comforts me

And puts everything in its place
So shush, my love,
Your look and your touch
Can leave everything unsaid
And I can face all those
Little people
Just like Gulliver did.
Thank you for being there, my love
At last I've found someone who's real
The maniacal choirs that screamed out a warning
Now sings out lullaby
The walls that crashed to bury you and me
Now shelter our hideaway
Thank you for being there my love
At last I've found someone that's real
Thank you for being there my love
At last I know that you're real.

Brian was musically light years ahead of the others in 1962, when he founded the Rolling Stones. He had an artistic talent for all things wonderful, and his favourite was music, music, music. The words 'unable to write music' regarding Brian have been flying on the banners of the establishment for decades now, with them preferring to treat the crowds like mushrooms: keep them in the dark and feed them dung.

Brian wrote songs from early on, and an early one by him is the Stones song for a Rice Krispies commercial in late 1963. Its title is *Wake Up in the Morning.* There are other songs by Brian that have been recorded by BBC, but not released, and two of them are *I Want You to Know* and *Dust My Pyramids*. He was vulnerable and afraid of the criticism from the Stones official song writers and management. Brian's songs were his secret and one of the few people that he would play his songs for was his girlfriend Linda, who explained that Brian did not feel threatened with her, for which reason he was comfortable to play his songs in her presence. Apparently he wanted to share his songs with the other Stones, but they were not welcome, so he returned home very depressed, and he always felt that other Stones did not want to know about his songs.

The Stones album *Aftermath* would have been a nice collection without Brian, but with him on *Paint It Black*, *Lady Jane* and *Under My Thumb* it became fabulous. It is more than likely that Brian wrote the music for his contributions; he had the skill, gift and passion for it. Why would he ever have been stupid enough to get involved in music, if it was an alien territory to him? Apparently, Marianne Faithfull says that *Ruby Tuesday* was essentially by Brian, which makes perfect sense, as Brian's recorder carries the melody. On the basis of song credits published the Stones members' memories says otherwise, but it does not sound surprising, considering various interests in the matter as well as memories fading.

There is also a most pathetic film *Mord und Totschlag*, if opinions are allowed, the only good aspect of which is the music Brian wrote. The film as such is a most unfortunate recording of acts by a so-called actress Anita Pallenberg way below the skills of Ronald Reagan in his heyday, and not surprisingly the film proved as unappreciated as it was unappealing at the Cannes Film Festival in 1967. Small wonder she was not nominated for an Oscar in the category of best actress in a foreign film. It seems reasonable to say the film director Volker Schlöndorff could have done better with expecting more from the actors, whom he could have chosen better, too, and the poor success of his low-quality production was definitely no fault of Brian's: the music is wonderful, with the theme repeated most beautifully throughout. The soundtrack was recorded between late 1966 and early 1967, and all music was composed, arranged and produced by Brian, with Glyn Johns' engineering. The soundtrack also featured session musicians Jimmy Page on guitar, Nicky Hopkins on piano, and Peter Gosling for background vocals. Brian played all other instruments, among of which were sitar, organ, recorder, banjo, harpsichord, autoharp, dulcimer, clarinet and harmonica. Although, and a cynic would say not surprisingly, comments on the internet are increasing to the extent that "it may be that Richards participated more than what was thought before." Perhaps give it another 5 or 10 years, and there will be a shift more and more in that direction, until the conclusion is reached that it was not Brian Jones who did any of it; wonders never cease and business is business.

It is obvious that Brian wrote music, despite being psychologically throttled by fellow Stones, as Brian kept complaining. His repertoire was far richer than the Stones standard from 1970 onward which is *'boom, boom boom, boom, ho, ho, ho, ho'*. It is amazing that other Stones seemingly wished to absorb credit for Brian's Moroccan tapes in July 1968, which was a time when the Stones apparently had no time for Brian and he was considered a burden. They spoke about engineer George Chkiantz being one of the first people to be heavily into phasing, and Brian then took his Joujouka tapes and put them through phasing, which was very much before its time. But other Stones then concluded it was an example of how adventurous the Stones were in that regard, although it was Brian doing it all. Why should credit not go to the person who does the job? Especially when Brian was not given any credit for his participation in song writing, even regarding Ruby Tuesday, on which his contribution is irreplaceable. [26]

It is well-known that manager Andrew Oldham wanted Richards and Jagger to do the song writing, and Brian was pushed out gradually. It seems most unlikely that any group would ever have a group member walk in with a finished song, for others to merely follow what is written for instruments used. Videos from Stones recording sessions do not support that thought either. Rather, songs emerged as mutual contributions perhaps on an idea, and the production was trial and error, as any creative work always will be. Why should it be different for Brian? Why should there have been other standards for Brian's music, amounting to the expectation that he was to produce a 'finished song' before others would look at it, to consider? One could only ever argue that group rules must be the same for everyone.

The only way to involve another person in what you are doing yourself is to invite him along and listen. Not talk but listen. Give the other one a chance. Do not sit around and wait the other one to approach you, because if you do that, you are ignoring the other person already and displaying a hostile attitude. If you want someone to join in, it will always be yours to invite, welcome and include, and it is not yours to sit and wait for someone to knock on your door and request an appointment. It is best to get off your backside and invite the other person in. Why should it be a one-way road with your rigid rules?

On top of which, Alexis Korner disagreed about the matter:

> "It's not true to say that Brian couldn't write music, but his reticence in putting his music forward for consideration by the group seems to have been due to a mixture of shyness and lack of confidence."

It most certainly seems that Brian's artistic talent went undetected and unappreciated. Writing a song always involves an artistic input, and art is not just short for Arthur. It is fine to think in those terms, if one so chooses, because we all make our choices and decide what doors to open for something new, and if and how often we open our minds to learn and develop. It is always an individual choice to open or close your mind, and everything has its consequences with pros and cons.

8
Brian Jones and Nicholas Fitzgerald

Nicholas Fitzgerald says he was a friend of Brian's, and there is no reason to disbelieve him more than any other person. He was born in 1948, an offspring of the massive Guinness fortune originating in Ireland, and a cousin to Tara Browne. Tara himself was a London socialite, and he became friends with Brian, both frequenting the London clubs and pubs for 1960s beautiful and psychedelic people. Nicholas, a fresh lad of only 17 at the time he met Brian, lived in Birmingham but visited London frequently. He was either homosexual or bisexual; he writes he was attracted to both guys and gals, and the moment he met Brian in July 1965, he fell in love with him, which in no way denotes anything sexual. But what he did write about his own sexuality, precious little as it was, is all in his book titled *Brian Jones: the inside story of the original Rolling Stone.* He writes that Brian asked him to stay the night on 2 July 1969, just to hold him, because he was scared at Cotchford. This has been twisted to him having had sex with Brian at Cotchford and that Brian was homosexual. Neither is true, and Brian was not homosexual. But what does it matter, if Brian was? Fitzgerald does talk about waking up one morning in the Kensington Palace Hotel in London, after a night out with Brian and some girls, as young women were called back then, and on that basis it seems there was a foursome in bed before the morning sun crept up to titillate the closed eyelids of those still in bed, for the sun to cast a shy shade of pale light on the groggy minds. Brian is known not to have minded group sex, and he obviously knew Nicholas was gay. So, he liked to flirt with young Nicholas, just to bring out blushing roses on those shy cheeks of the young lad, confused with his sexuality.

But Brian himself was not gay. Brian was a heterosexual who liked women very much indeed, and that was the direction where his testosterone headed every time the thought of sex hit his mind, and we know it hits the mind of everyone all the time. He talked about these matters with Nicholas, interestingly saying that he thinks most people are ambidextrous in their sexuality but have trouble letting go on grounds of being too inhibited with what they have learnt they should be like. This misinterpretation, wilful or otherwise, has further contributed to the misunderstanding that Brian were gay. Whatever his preferences may have been, his goings-on with more than one partner seem to have involved a woman every time, and homosexuality is no longer the issue it was 60 years ago. But, Nicholas and Brian remained friends until 2 July 1969, and Nicholas' book was published fourteen years later in 1985. Sadly, it has almost fallen into oblivion with several more recent books published about Brian Jones and his life.

Typically, the book has been dismissed as pure fiction. After Brian's death, Fitzgerald went to the police a number of times to talk about the matter, but he did not want to make a witness statement. That has been regarded as proof for him being an odd-ball seeking attention but only wasting other people's time. A further criterion used against him is that he wrote most of the book in the form of a dialogue. This alone proves, the arguments go, that the book is rubbish, because it is not possible that he would remember what was said between individuals years later.

Now, the complication arises that he never said he wrote nonfiction, typically understood to be facts. The book contains discussions between himself and members of the Stones, Marianne Faithfull, Anita Pallenberg, Eric Easton, Suki Potier, Tara Browne, Andrew Oldham and many others, all attending events, pubs and recordings of TV-shows. Fitzgerald obviously had the methodological problem how to present in writing what different people were chatting about. How would one present a scene that involves many people in attendance, talking to each other and throwing in comments, if there is no dialogue? Obviously, dialogue is the only way to go. But for some reason people assume nonfiction means that everything written has factually happened, in contrast to which fiction is fantasy with no connection to reality.

Another mistake is to assume that actual events must be presented in a third person narrative. More fool those who do that. The method of writing in dialogue is traditional, and it has been used in the history of literature ever since spoken content was included in writing. It is a practical way to convey a message. The form of a dialogue to pass on information does not impair the value of the content provided, especially when the details fall in place with information from other sources and tally with events known. Fitzgerald's book closest falls in the category of nonfiction, because it is based on real events that occurred. It is self-evident that the discussions are not a word for word relay of what was said, and there is no need for them to be so; it is the message that matters and not the precise wording. Fitzgerald did not say he was repeating exact comments made or that he memorized what was said. Such a claim would have been ridiculous. Although Anna Wohlin did claim exactly that regarding her alleged conversations with Brian, and she then reproduced the allegedly memorized discussions in her book published in 1999.

A further criterion against Fitzgerald is that the Stones members apparently claim they cannot remember a person by that name in their 1960s history. But remember the book came out in 1985, and Fitzgerald wrote that a man matching Keylock's description growled at him and his friend Richard Cadbury to get out of Cotchford on 2 July 1969. He did not know the man's name, and Keylock is not mentioned in his book. However, Keylock referred to Fitzgerald by his name, so Keylock knew about him. Fitzgerald later recognized Keylock's voice at Hyde Park on 5 July, but he still did not know his name. He did not know that the man who shouted at him at Cotchford on 2 July was called Keylock, and Keylock did not admit he was there until 2009. It is possible Fitzgerald found out about Keylock's admission, because Keylock died on 2 July 2009 and Fitzgerald on 3 October also in 2009. It would make sense that the Stones would not admit any knowledge of Fitzgerald, because he is the only person with a witness account of the way Brian was killed. Apart from Brian, no participant in the events of 2 July 1969 knew that Fitzgerald would be arriving later that night, and Brian did not know what time he was going to arrive either. Also, Fitzgerald obviously had a good reason not to sign a witness statement, and that was to protect his life, because any connection with Brian in 1969 turned out a dangerous business afterwards.

Fitzgerald features in the chapters to follow, and there is every reason to think he was telling the truth. He unwittingly became the only witness to how Brian Jones died. Which was not because Brian fell asleep, while having a swim.

9
Was It a Premature Death?

The Bridge of San Luis Ray is a powerful book for anyone who knows the world is round and then continues to think we are born as a random meeting of sperm and ovum, after which the gravity forces their travel downwards to occupy the uterus as joint tenants. The ensuing life story ends with whatever happens to be in place for the final curtain fall, to end the existence of the accidental individual in the universe, and then there is nothing. It is the popular Darwinistic mode of thinking, particularly popular among younger generations and healthy people. Even then it has always had its ideological recalcitrants, and ultimately there are no atheists in foxholes.

The challenges the book brings to the scientific, modern rationale rampant in societies are profound, and they affect theories about religion, cause and effect, philosophy and all streams of life. The book's mixture of the spiritual with the humane is directly connected to the theories and understandings of Brian's drowning on 2 July 1969, whether his passing was a murder or not, and the reader so willing, it will challenge the thought that Brian passed away too early. Essentially, the fact that people consider an event unforeseen does not mean it was so, because who lives and who dies is not in the hands of humans, except in cases of murder. And they, too, might serve the purpose for a force originating in realms unknown to mere mortals.

The Bridge of San Luis Ray was written by Thornton Wilder (1897–1975), an American playwright and Pulitzer Prize winner three times over. It is considered one of the major achievements in American literature. Wilder started writing it in 1926 and won his first Pulitzer Prize for it in 1927, by which time it had been through seventeen printings and sold ca. 300,000 copies. It has never been out of print, and its themes will remain topical as long as the world continues to exist. The book is about a very fine bridge in Peru, fictitious as the bridge is, falling down into the gulf below, killing five travellers on it in 1714. That the fine bridge should fall went against all expectations it should occur ever, because it was an excellent, respected bridge and much admired by the locals. It was very much a bridge over troubled waters in being essential for local travel across the waters underneath. It was considered strong and non-collapsible, much in the way *the Titanic* was considered unsinkable, and when the bridge did collapse, and *the Titanic* did sink, there arose a huge calamity how that could happen.

The collapse of the bridge was witnessed by a monk called Brother Juniper, who then set about to establish how it could be that such a catastrophic event should occur against all expectations, and he delved into the past of those five who lost their lives. Despite the investigation taking several years to complete, and himself being killed, Brother Juniper did find out the events of each individual's life before they proceeded to the bridge to cross it. However, discussing what those events were would not only be irrelevant here, but would also amount to a plot spoiler; it is always better to read the original source, which, in this case, is an exceptional book.

What Thornton Wilder was actually writing about was the existence or non-existence of spiritual or divine invention of what human life entails, if it does, and the essence of love in its manifestations. He explored issues of the stabilizing influence of constancy in life, symbolized by the bridge before collapse, and the uncertainty of life playing havoc in peoples' minds, symbolized by the tragedy of the collapse. Globally and in reality, contemporary people faced these existential and philosophical issues in the events of September 11, and they continue to be affected by the events. In a single moment, the collapse of the bridge of San Lui Rey in 1714 changed life for those around, as did the collapse of the Twin Towers on September 11, 2001, and as did the drowning of Brian Jones at Cotchford on 2 July 1969.

Brian was looking for a property outside greater London, in a more peaceful place, but still within a comfortable travelling distance from London. He wanted a complete change of lifestyle with farm animals and a new future with growing his own food. It was far more a vision of a farmer in the country instead of a famous rock-n-roller having a weekend to visit his property outside London. He had firm plans for a new life altogether. He had set his mind on Nansladron Farm just off B3273 near Pentewan in Southern Cornwall. He talks about it in a newspaper or magazine interview likely to have been in the spring or summer of 1968; Brian found Cotchford farm in Hartfield, Sussex, in August 1968, so his plans to buy Nansdorf must have been before that.[27] He said that he wanted to buy a farm to become self-sufficient, with the British economy seemingly collapsing anytime soon. He wanted to grow all his food and be independent of suppliers. He was wanting to have cattle, pigs and chicken, and the property run by a farm manager. He was intending to commute to London and spend most of his time at his country property. He was also looking forward to some fishing, with the property close to the sea.

In another interview titled *The economy is a joke* around early June 1968, as it must have been, because Brian refers to 'the new single Jumping Jack Flash' released on 24 May 1968, he talks about his concerns for the British economy:

> "The economy is a joke nowadays. I must be self-sufficient and able to do without money. It is so peaceful down there with the sea so close. It is such a paradoxical situation. Here I am, hung up on electronic music, London and the pop scene, and there I want to go and live in the country. I guess I would become a commuter..."[28]

Brian bought Cotchford on 21 November 1968 and gradually moved in, but he continued to travel to London as required and as he wished. His life since Pallenberg, Richards and Jagger had abandoned him in Morocco in March 1967 had been one of misery, suffering and destruction, both mental and physical. The drug busts and the police haunting him exacerbated his distress and suffering. He felt unwelcome and unwanted by the other Stones members, which he undoubtedly was; he had been gradually ousted with nobody standing up to help or support him. That those who did not participate in it directly does not even remotely suggest they should qualify for applause, because they ignored Brian being mistreated, thereby allowing it to continue. What is right is usually not the popular and easy way, but shedding tears decades later does nothing to undo wrong knowingly done, when you had the opportunity to do the right thing in the first place; standing for right when it is unpopular is the test of character. Visiting Brian's grave now does nothing to help Brian, although it may help to lessen the visitor's burden of guilt, with money already safely in the bank and no risk to the visitor's own comfort.

Having said that, Bill Wyman deserves full credit for bringing up the truth about the origins of the Rolling Stones and Brian Jones as the founder of the Rolling Stones, as he did on the documentary *The Stones and Brian Jones* which aired on BBC2 on 15 May 2023.

Daunting and miserable as the months and two years for Brian were since March 1967, there was a new and more peaceful future ahead for him at Cotchford. It was meant to be the beginning of a new life for him, with doors closed to the past pain he experienced with the Rolling Stones. He had also been receiving psychiatric counselling and medication, and was on the mend from his excessive use of drugs and alcohol. He had had a problem with alcohol since his teenage years, and it would have eased the pain from his mistreatment at home in Cheltenham. Yet he continued drinking heavily all his life, as well as smoking equally heavily, which was common in the 1960s. Apparently he had plans to start a new group, but there is no way of verifying what might have been the actual case over 50 years ago. The important issues are that Brian had broken free from the Stones organization and was starting afresh as soon as he paid off the workers at Cotchford doing renovations. His future lay ahead, and he was working to discontinue taking drugs, but was still continuing with excessive alcohol. He had travelled a long road to get where he was on the morning of 2 July 1969, and that was at Cotchford: his safe haven, the domicile of his new life, with his music room furnished and furbished for his new practices and plans. And then he drowned later that night, in the swimming pool of his own safe haven, with his life abruptly and violently taken from him.

This is where the *Bridge of San Luis Rey* raises its head again. The issues that troubled the mind of Thornton Wilder in the early 1920s were echoed, and continue to be echoed, in the minds of millions of others. The rational man of today is likely to consider that Brian Jones' life was cut short by an unforeseen tragedy. The Cotchford grounds of a safe haven and a new beginning turned into a disaster zone that deprived him of his life too soon, the modern man of rationalism will say. Like the collapsed bridge that represented constancy, safety and continuation turned into a place of horror that abruptly cut lives short, so did Cotchford turn from a safe haven to a tragic scene where Brian's life was cut short. Yet the places remained the same; what changed was people's perception and understanding of them. Was it a mere coincidence that the bridge collapsed and killed those people, or would they have been killed anyway in different circumstances, had they chosen not to cross the bridge? Equally, was it a mere coincidence that Brian was killed at Cotchford, or would he have been killed anyway in different circumstances, had he bought another property without a swimming pool? The first property he intended to buy at Nandorn, Cornwall, did not have a swimming pool, but it was close to the sea, swimming and fishing. It is not known, why Brian changed his mind. – Kindly do not flare up, claiming this goes way past the Rolling Stones and rock' n roll, because the matter is about life and death as people perceive them. And believe it or not, even the Rolling Stones are subject to life and death and the laws of nature, and not vice versa.

The modern, rational man in his technically equipped surroundings is likely to remain convinced that life is meant to be the way modern, rational man thinks it should be, considering all medical advancements made, and ensuring there is a thick wad of extra cash in the pocket for the bus fares of the surviving dear ones, or even if they are not so dear ones, on top of a comfortable bank balance or investments galore. The modern, rational man then reaches the age of 90, as was the case before COVID-19, and he then gradually fades away in a care place neatly located in a leafy, green suburb, where he enjoys salmon and béarnaise sauce for lunch and roast beef for dinner. His life will end peacefully with him lying horizontally between fresh sheets and the sun going down behind the trees.

Such illusions, not lasting long in any society ever, were blown away with COVID-19 throwing spanners in the wheels of such an egocentric understanding of life. A critical mind would understand that it was fake and flawed from the start. But the modern, rational mind focuses on the comfort desired and already achieved, and will maintain that matters have gone wrong, when such a life expectancy is not reached. If somebody's life ends abruptly, horribly, violently or painfully, the person's life has been cut short, yet the beginning of life is exactly like that; birth can be abrupt, horrible, violent and always painful at least for the mother, and we do not know what it is like for the child being born.

While none of those attributes may be desirable, they are the reality of life.

And what if Brian's life was as long as it was meant to be? What if it was not cut short but ran as long as was written down in the Great Plan of All Things? What if Brian had already completed what was deemed for him in the Celestial Records? Yes, it is likely he wanted more, but perhaps he needed no more; we do not get to make the choices. Perhaps he had already found what he needed to find, and Cotchford had already gifted him with the message he was there for. What we tangibly do is the mere façade of the steps required in our life. Perhaps Brian had already found again who he was originally, before human actions of unlove catapulted him out of Cheltenham, Gloucestershire, to find another him that someone would love. As long as that lad from his childhood remained unloved, he was adrift without direction. And it just may be that all was well for him on the level of life force, although we modern humans see things differently and we believe our illusion.

As if we ever knew what to focus on in life to start off with, and people continue to think that travel broadens the mind. What is perceived as important is to maximize the number of experiences gained, on the assumption it is an important criterion for a young person making future plans or an older person contemplating about his achievements in life, so a-travelling we go, to broaden our minds. Yet broadening does nothing in terms of depth gained any better than walking on sandy beaches stretching for miles does, because with every step we take on a sandy beach, the experience remains the same and the sea we admire the same shallow water washing up on the shore. For an understanding of life, a travel on foot down a footpath in a park can be most rewarding, if you keep your eyes open and really look at what is around.

With that argument perhaps not too attractive for the reader, it is good to have a look at Brian's physical realities of his desired peaceful life based at Cotchford. And we can do so, because we have the autopsy report of 5 July 1969. Studying the details, even a lay person quickly establishes that Brian was not a physically healthy man. He was only 27, but there were several concerns; his inner organs were in serious trouble.

The autopsy report refers to the brain as "congested and oedematous. Punctate haemorrhages in white matter." The average weight of an adult male brain is ca. 1400g, so the weight of 1553g in the autopsy report is slightly more than the average. The swelling of the brain could be due to damage during drowning, but it can also occur after a long and intensive drug use. The slight swelling of the brain has not caused much concern among those interested in Brian Jones' drowning, but the punctate haemorrhages in the white matter continues to be a favourite in the argument that Brian was beaten up and his head was shaken in an act of violence. The reasoning behind this argument is that such haemorrhages occur in infants who have been shaken severely, causing the baby's head to move violently back and forth, and the ensuing damage is called the *Shaken Baby Syndrome*. It can also occur in adults, then being called the *Shaken Adult Syndrome*. But an adult person cannot shake another adult in the way an adult person can shake a baby, so the theory does not work. Also, adult victims identified as suffering from the syndrome were also diagnosed with bruising in different parts of the body, skin abrasions, head injuries and damaged teeth. These people were physically abused and assaulted, and there was abundant physical proof of that.

Yet Brian had no such damage on his body, and it is reasonable to say that if he had been attacked physically, there would have been signs of it on his body. The likelihood of a physical assault that leaves no physical marks is non-existent; you cannot beat up someone and leave no sign of it, unless you take extreme precautions in artificial settings. The autopsy report contains absolutely nothing to suggest there was a physical assault on Brian.

However, there is another, and a far more likely reason for those small haemorrhages, and that is drugs and alcohol. What exacerbates the likelihood of those being the culprit is the improbability that Brian's body would have remained unharmed from his extensive use of alcohol and drugs, and among substances that can cause brain damage are alcohol, barbiturates, cocaine, amphetamines, LSD, heroin and marijuana. It is not reasonable to argue that while these drugs are known to have an effect on the human brain, it would not have happened with Brian. And Brian, sadly, had used them all.

His lungs were rather normal in size, and it seems he had pleurisy. Pleurisy is an inflammation of pleura in the chest cavity. With pleurisy, a small amount of fluid normally present in your chest cavity is absent; a normal person has each lung covered by a thin membrane called visceral pleura, and a similar membrane, called parietal pleura, covers the inner wall of the chest, exactly like a sandwich has two sides with a filling between them. In this space between the chest wall and the lung surface there should be a small amount of fluid, which allows the lungs to expand and contract in a smooth, sliding movement during breathing. But Brian did not have any fluid in that small space, and some of the symptoms of the condition are frequent coughing, breathing problems and generally feeling unwell, as was often the case with Brian. They may well have been ignored as a potential cause for pleurisy, because they are also symptoms of asthma. Further, in the space where a healthy person would have some fluid but Brian did not, there were adhesions from the left lung to the chest wall, and this means perhaps scar tissue where there was some unnatural damage; such adhesions are abnormal formations of fibrous materials inside the body. These adhesions are painful and they may become cancerous. They needed urgent attention and determination of the cause including treatment for them, but to establish what they were, a biopsy was needed. The autopsy report does not mention the amount of the adhesions or their size, but, it is fair to say it no longer mattered at the time. But Brian would have needed to consult a specialist in thoracoscopy, to learn what the adhesions were, if they were to be diagnosed ever. It would have taken several visits to medical specialists and a lot of anxiety.

The origins of thoracoscopy go back to 1910, when it was introduced for the treatment of tuberculosis, to remove or destroy adhesions to gain access to the area between the plura; remember the lining outside the lung on the one side and the lining of the chest cavity on the other, the sandwich model? In tuberculosis, air can accumulate in that small space between the two, and if not removed, the accumulated air can make the lung collapse under the pressure. Methods involved were mostly discontinued after the 1950s, because with the treatment of tuberculosis becoming available, the use of thoracoscopy declined, although it continued to be used in continental Europe.

Later, matters changed drastically in the early 1990s, with laparoscopic procedures becoming available and widely used in medical procedures, and these days there is no end to the development of easy procedures to gain access into the body cavity. But even 1991 was 22 years after Brian's passing. While it is impossible to say what may have been available for Brian, it seems that he may have been in the process of developing lung cancer, being the heavy smoker he was. Time was not on Brian's side. He needed medical attention to the symptoms and continuing chest pain he undoubtedly had, and it was more complicated than asthma.

At post-mortem, Brian's heart weighed 411g, and was thereby heavier than the high-end variation of average heart weight of 340g for an adult male. The human heart has a left chamber and a right chamber, or a left atrium and a right one, and each side of Brian's heart was dilated i.e. enlarged. What happens with an enlarged heart is that with the chamber getting bigger, the muscular wall stretches and becomes thinner and weaker. Such a thinner and weaker muscle, also called a flabby muscle, is effectively stretched too far and it no longer has the power to contract as it should. Consequently, the heart is not able to pump a sufficient amount of oxygen-rich blood into the body's circulation. What that means is that Brian may have had a heart disease called dilated cardiomyopathy. The condition can be narrowed down to the term alcoholic cardiomyopathy, but it is hard to say whether it applied in Brian's case. Be that as it may, it is a very unpleasant condition to have, and Brian possibly had a high blood pressure, only to add to the array of health problems he had.

Help for high blood pressure was already available, with the first medication for it out in the early 1960s, when the British physician James W. Black developed beta blockers for the treatment of angina, and they had the lovely side effect that they turned out to lower blood pressure, too. But in terms of Brian's symptoms of dilated cardiopathy, only complete abstinence from alcohol could help. Without the abstinence, even today, the 4-year mortality rate is as high as 50%, and life expectancy is not more than 10 years after the onset of the condition. To continue with his life, Brian either had to stop alcohol completely, or probably get a heart transplant at some stage. It seems the first was not happening, so it is likely to have turned out a matter of a heart transplant, given some time.

As we know, the first heart transplant on a human being was performed by Christiaan Barnard in Capetown, South Africa, in December 1967. The patient lived 18 days post-surgery. Since then, an estimated 150,000 people worldwide have benefited from a heart transplant, being able to return to a nearly normal quality of life. The average number of years the patients have gained is 14. It is reasonable to say it is unlikely that Brian would have benefitted a particularly long time in or after 1969, because the procedure was still in its pioneering stages with more problems to overcome than already solved. Brian would have had to go overseas for the operation, because the first heart transplant with a long-term success in Britain was performed in August 1979. That is 10 years after Brian's passing, and it is highly unlikely he would have had the health to wait that long. Further, there is the high likelihood that doctors would not have been able to operate on him, because his general physical condition was very poor. Again, time was not on Brian's side, to postpone drastic measures to aid his poor physical health, which were unlikely to be available back then.

The biggest and most alarming issue in the autopsy report is perhaps the severe dysfunction of his enormously enlarged, fatty liver; a normal weight of the liver of an adult male is ca. 1650g, and Brian's liver weighed a huge 3000g. A liver being enlarged is one thing, and it being fatty is another, but neither of them is good news. Fatty liver develops as a result of large alcohol consumption, and Brian had had years of it, having started in his teens. Fatty liver is the first stage of alcohol-related liver disease (ARLD) and an undeniable symptom of excessive drinking; your body is saying it cannot cope with what you are putting into it. Enlarged liver, on the other hand, is not a disease as such, but a sign of a serious medical problem, such as liver disease (fatty liver is a liver disease), congestive heart failure or cancer. Out of those three Brian had a liver disease, congestive heart failure (his heart was enlarged and flabby, trying to pump blood well enough trying to give the body a normal supply), and his body may have been on way to develop lung cancer, which those adhesions in his chest cavity may have been a sign of.

It could also be that his liver was swollen with inflammation, which is the next stage of ARLD, and that would occur after years of excessive drinking and use of drugs. This inflammation is called alcoholic hepatitis, and it causes your liver to become inflamed and swollen. From there, the next stage is cirrhosis, and that is fatal. Brian was not there yet, but the pathologist's report notes that the liver was severely dysfunctional and chronically troubled, and the life expectancy with a fatty liver disease is less than five years. Or less, because with a health problem of that magnitude, combined with other issues Brian had, his heart and lungs were likely to become more than a serious problem.

The other organs also had problems, with the spleen and kidneys being congested, i.e., not working as they should. There was not much urine present in the bladder, and the kidneys were congested, and at 190g and 181g larger than normal ca.130–140g. The difference in size was perhaps due to swelling, caused by the build-up of urine in the kidney, because there is an obstruction preventing drainage to the bladder. That obstruction need not be anything other than poor blood circulation not allowing kidneys to work normally. It can also occur concurrently with liver dysfunction, which Brian also had. But like the kidneys, the spleen, too, was enlarged and congested. Enlarged spleen is not a problem as such, but it being congested is likely to be due to an infection or a liver disease.

Had Brian been able to live longer from his liver's point of view, he would perhaps have required a liver transplant, which raises the question what the way and likelihood of that were in England at the time. And the likelihood of that happening was essentially non-existing. The first successful liver transplant operation in Europe was by Sir Roy Calne and Roger Williams in Cambridge in 1968, successful in the meaning that the young patient lived some 18 months after the operation. But it was very much the early days in the field, and liver transplants were a very rare thing in early 1970s, further complicated with the problem of lack of storage techniques for preserving the liver until the operation. It was not until 1976 that methods permitting reasonably long storage were developed, so clinical trials could start. And there would have remained the obstacle that Brian would have had to stop alcohol entirely to qualify being on the programme. Again, time was not on Brian's side.

Brian had many visitors to Cotchford in his last two months, most of them not friends but acquaintances of some sort, but some had known him long enough to be able to comment on his mental health and ability to move about or play music, as opposed to what those abilities used to be for Brian. Good friends that remained beyond June 1969 were musician Alexis Korner and his wife Bobbie. Korner was involved in music all his life, going through various phases with various people outside the scope of this book, and in 1968–1969 he formed another group of aspiring young musicians with his daughter Sappho and Nick South, a friend of Korner's son Nico. Korner, together with his wife and his band, went over to Cothcford a number of times in the early summer of 1969, in preparation for the group to perform with Brian in Europe in July that year.

But a most striking problem emerged, and it was that Brian would not play guitar no matter how often or kindly he was asked to. He would not be cajoled into doing it by Korner either. Nick South found that Brian did not look too well, and it looked he habitually consumed a few bottles of wine daily, looking bleary. Nick South felt that judging by appearances, Brian was trying to cope and survive, lacking alertness for things around him.[29]

Korner also asked his friend John Mayall to come along to Cotchford, and Mayall with his wife and two children visited Brian on 30 June, just 2 days before Brian's passing.

Brian looked very unwell, having trouble walking without supporting himself on something. A shadow of his former self, he was still excited about putting new music together, but he no longer had sense of rhythm and time, which was upsetting to Mayal. However, Mayall encouraged Brian to continue with his plans for making new music, because he was obviously enthusiastic about it.[30]

It is difficult to argue against the views of such experienced and capable musicians as Korner and Mayall, and with them both visiting Brian in person, they were offering first-hand experiences. Proceeding on that ground, it is reasonable to say that Brian no longer had the extraordinary skill to play any musical instrument he picked up as he used to, which was unlike any other musician at the time. And perhaps he no longer could play any musical instrument at all, or if he still had the skill to play some, he was not able to play guitar, which was the number one instrument he had been playing since he had learnt to play an instrument. Guitar was his number one instrument in his Rolling Stones group, and the early Stones years became a success with Brian on guitar. But no longer at Cotchford in June 1969. It seems like something had ended.

An interesting matter is the 'super-group' of sorts Brian allegedly was wanting to start. It has been speculated on extensively, with essentially very little proof available. It is mentioned in at least two sources, the first one being his friend Nicholas Fitzgerald's book. According to Fitzgerald, Brian told him in 1969 that towards the end of 1968, there were four musicians making a trial recording for the Beatles' label *Apple*. Those four musicians played under the group name *Balls*, and one of those musicians was John Lennon and another one was Brian. Brian told that the other two swore him to secrecy, so all Brian was disclosing was that one was a lead guitar and the other one a drummer. Apparently the foursome recorded one track called *Go to the Mountains*. Brian also spoke about perhaps teaming up with Jimi Hendrix. But he was very concerned that he would not be allowed to enter the US, after losing his drug appeal, and he very much liked the US and hoped to be able to continue to visit the continent.[31]

Whether the guitar player referred to above was Jimi Hendrix or not, Bill Wyman and the Brian Jones documentary aired on 15 May 2023 on BBC 2 quite unexpectedly provide interesting information on the matter. Wyman, in an almost furtive manner, as if he were not supposed to be saying what he did say, which is talk about Brian Jones playing with Jimi Hendrix, unexpectedly turns to someone sitting beside him but off camera, and enquires what he should say. He continues to make a comment that nobody knows about Brian and Jimi playing together, after which there is a short video clip of the two doing exactly that. To add further confusion for the surprised viewer, munching on his popcorn and rolling his eyes, a text then appears to say they often played together, but it is not verbalised by Wyman or anyone else. Yet apparently there are people who do know, including the person Wyman enquired with, that there was a strong connection between Brian and Jimi Hendrix, and they were in the habit of playing together. What else is there one is not allowed to say? Especially because these matters are connected with circumstances around Brian's death, so why the secrecy? Whose rules are these?

Fitzgerald also writes that Brian called him again on 5 May 1969, which was 3 days before Allen Klein and the Beatles signed their management contract. Brian sounded nervous and jumpy on hearing the news, and wanted to know if Fitzgerald had told anyone about Brian starting a new group. Apparently Alexis Korner had pointed out to Brian that it could be dangerous if people learnt about this plan of Brian's. Brian said that if certain people believed Brian and Lennon were teaming up, they might get jittery. It could be a threat to both the Stones and the Beatles, and that could cost a lot of people a lot of money.[32] The drummer he referred to is likely to be Mitch Mitchell of the Jimi Hendrix Experience and Noel Redding, a bass player with the same group. The drummer could also have been Micky Waller. Noel Redding quit the Jimi Hendrix experience either on 29 June or 1 July 1969, and Micky Waller was also available at the time.

Another source bringing up the issue of a new group and Brian's potential future in the music business is a German teen magazine called BRAVO.[33] Thomas Beyel, one of its reporters, visited Brian in London in June 1969, and the article was published on 16 June. Before that, Brian had announced his departure from the Rolling Stones on 9 June with newspapers reporting him saying that he no longer sees eye-to-eye with the others over the music produced. He wanted to play his kind of music, which was not the Stones music anymore. The music Jagger and Richards had been writing had progressed at a tangent. According to Brian, they had a friendly meeting and agreed that a termination, be it temporary or permanent, was the only solution.

In the BRAVO article, Thomas Beyel describes travelling to London on hearing news that Brian should have left the

Stones. He is wanting to talk to the Stones and Brian, to establish if it is true. On arrival in London, he goes to the Stones Head Quarters in Maddock Street, where Mick, Bill, Keith and Charlie are about to be rushed off to an appointment. With the other Stones out of the office, Beyel turns to Tom Keylock and insists that Keylock tell him if the news about Brian are true. Keylock then discloses to him that Brian is staying with a friend in London, and lets Beyel call Brian. Brian answers the phone in a sleepy voice, and after agreeing to see Beyel, he wants to talk to Keylock. Arrangements are made for Keylock to take Beyel to Brian's hide-away after dark, and Beyel interviews Brian and also listens to some of Brian's new music. The essential regarding the split-up between Brian and the other Stones appears below in an English translation.

Jones: So you want to hear the truth from me. Well then, the old Stones sound is not what I like anymore. I think it is a thing of the past. I would like to write and play my own music. After friendly discussions, we came to the conclusion that separation is the only solution there is. Happy with that?

Beyel asks if there is any chance that the Stones might get together again.

Jones: None whatsoever. I wanted to leave over two years ago, but Mick convinced me to stay. But there is no going back anymore.

Brian looks pale, exhausted and unwell, and not at all happy. Beyel encourages Brian, and tells him that fans would miss him, and the Stones are planning a tour again.

Jones: Tell them that I will soon be back with my own group. It will be decided in the next few weeks. Perhaps I will only produce music. One thing I know for sure: I would like to become rich, finally lay my hands on big money, like Mick and Keith...

Brian jumps up, rummages through his box of records and retrieves an album with the words *JouJouka* on the cover.

Jones: I produced that in Algeria: my first LP. Would you like to hear it? It is genuine African folk music. Recorded in the streets in the middle of the night.

They listen to the music together.

Jones: This is music. I will be composing in this style.

Brian is very excited about the music, but Beyel is not, and he leaves Brian's hide-away unconvinced about Brian's new music.

Both the Alexis Korner and the BRAVO magazine accounts are interesting, but with Jones, Hendrix and Lennon all gone decades ago, it is difficult to authenticate what precisely holds true. There is also a gap of at least six months between the trial recording in late 1968, as mentioned by Brian in Fitzgerald's book, and the BRAVO interview in June 1969. It is likely that during that time Brian and Hendrix also played together.

A plan involving Brian and John Lennon would have had the problem that Lennon was apparently no special friend of Brian's, and he did not hold Brian in high regard like George Harrison did. Which does not mean he would not have been capable and willing to work with Brian. He expressed his disgust at the waste of Brian dying in the way he did, but he did not run down Brian in his comments, as is often suggested. In July 1969, Lennon was still part of the Beatles until the Beatles broke up in September, a good two months after

Brian's passing. After the Beatles break-up, Lennon gradually spent more and more time in the US, until he moved there permanently in August 1971.

Jimi Hendrix, on the other hand, was a good friend of Brian's, especially in 1967 but also later, by all accounts. Then Hendrix passed away in September 1970, a mere 14 months after Brian did, so even if Brian had lived, a 'super group' with Hendrix would not have lasted very long. Further, Brian could not get a visa to enter USA, so they would have had to practice and perform in the UK at least until such time that Brian was allowed to enter the US again. Also, as discussed earlier, Alexis Korner, Nick South and John Mayall all said that there seem to have been valid issues with Brian's ability to produce music, and he would not touch a guitar. If there ever was a plan of a 'super group' and Brian had lived longer, it would have fallen apart with Jimi Hendrix' passing away. On top of which, Brian's health problems were significant and he would have had to focus on them, rather than anything else.

What certainly seems to be the case is that Brian had a wish, intent and desire to produce his own music, and that may be as far as things got before early July 1969; it does take time to plan, discuss and ponder together with others you may wish to work with. And it also seems that Brian had not produced any essential amount of music at Cothcford, because the music he played to the BRAVO reporter were the Pipes of JouJouka, or an earlier version of the album that was published for him posthumously. On top of which Brian spent a lot of time in London away from Cotchford in June, mulling things over in his secret hidey-hole, which may have been Nicholas Fitzgerald's place in London.

But as we can see, there were many factors at play regarding Brian's future after he had found Cotchford and was settling down there for a new future. On the basis of the autopsy report, he had essentially major issues with too many organs in his chest and abdominal cavities to suggest a life span of more than perhaps 5 years, or perhaps 10. He needed total abstinence from alcohol, drugs and smoking straight away, and that failing, organ transplants were a theoretical possibility at some point in time. It is fair to say that total abstinence was more than unlikely to happen in Brian's case. For that to occur, he had to change his lifestyle completely, and while he seemingly was prepared to change, him actually doing that is very inconsistent with the person he was. So far, he had not managed to do it. That alone would have been depressing, and he already had mental issues and strong mood swings. As far as can be understood, he was continuing in the care of medical professionals. We do not know exactly how much he knew about his failing physical condition, but Zou Zou, a girl-friend he used to be involved with around 1965, recently spoke about it to shed some light on the matter. She described Brian being in a really bad shape and needing help. According to her, it was only some 3 weeks before Brian's drowning that he told her about asking Mick to take him to the hospital, apparently because he knew he was so unwell that he could not go on.[34]

There are no grounds to suggest that his doctors did not inform him of his poor physical health, so the likelihood is that he was well aware of his physical health failing. He was always a bright and intelligent person and wanted to know what was going on. There is no suggestion here that his death was a suicide, because throwing a party with arguments and a lot of commotion is not the way one would do it, if one wanted to. The pool was there every day, and Brian could have slipped away quietly anytime he wanted to. But apparently he did not, and apparently it was no accident either. Yet all the intrigue and planning in preparation for his apparent murder seems futile, because it is most likely he would not have lived much longer, with a steady decline in his abilities possibly on a monthly basis. Bearing that in mind, and considering how emotionally burdensome it would have been for him to know his physical decline at such a young age, it is easy to understand that he appeared tired and unsteady to those who visited him at Cothcford.

While it seems almost certain that he was murdered on that fateful night of 2 July 1969, it seems that all things in life came to a head for Brian Jones at Cotchford. The Stones manager Allen Klein was also the manager for the Beatles in 1969; he was given a 3-year contract for the position on 8 May 1969. He was in London Town in early July for Rolling Stones business and probably for Beatles business as well. Brian had the popularity, his own name and the Rolling Stones name, although not in legal terms, but it would have been impossible to wrench the right to use the name off him, because it was him who chose it for his Rolling Stones in 1962. The Beatles were still a group together, and Klein undoubtedly wanted to protect his large business interests in the matter. Neither he nor the Beatles knew at the time that the group was going to break up in late September 1969 and Lennon would be heading for the USA, although he could clearly see there were problems. Keylock told Klein about Brian's enthusiastic plans for a Jones & Lennon partnership in 1969, and it did not go down well with Klein.

In fact, he was apparently furious that Lennon would leave the Beatles and the Stones would be suffering from Brian inadvertently stealing the limelight and business from the Stones. Not because Brian ever intended it that way, but because his musical contributions, appearances and style were always the magnet to draw crowds to the Stones concerts and their music. Girls wanted him and guys wanted him more than they wanted the other Stones put together. So no, Klein did absolutely not want competition from Brian in any shape or form. Why would the other Stones want it either, considering they were apparently facing financial ruin in 1969? Whatever money there was to flow in had to go towards Klein and his protégés. Brian was a major financial threat. But what Klein, Keylock or anyone else in the respective organizations did not know of was the dismal state of Brian's physical health.

Frank Thorogood and his builders were wanting more money from Brian, and apparently a permanent stay at Cothford as well, where they would hang around until the property was sold. Like the others whose cold interests were against Brian, they did not know about Brian's failing physical health. It seems all factors around Brian's life reached their zenith in the early summer of 1969. All things considered, it seems impossible there was going to be a future for him, unless he was willing to disappear and not have any plans other than sheep farming at John O'Groats. And with those around Brian not getting what they wanted, or saw a real threat in him, the solution was to engage bullies with a Dalek attitude and exterminate. And exterminate they did. The roads Brian had travelled led to their end station at Cotchford on 2 July 1969, and Cotchford became Brian's Bridge of San Luis Ray.

Brian Jones claimed many times that people were after him to kill him. He was dreading being killed. How convenient for all those whose business interests ran contrary to those of Brian that Brian died just before he was going to move onward and a huge payment was apparently due to him from the Stones organization on 3 July! Realistically, had Brian not died when he did, all those others would have faced a less lucrative future and severe competition, because Brian was highly popular with the public. – But oh goodness gracious me: a sudden, deep concern arises! Best glance quickly sideways in a furtive manner to ask the wall: 'What should I say? Am I allowed to say that'? And the wall, silently, nods in response, and a telepathic message is sent and received to perhaps include it in a footnote.

One likes to think that perhaps earlier, in quiet moments, Brian sat outside and thought about his life so far; who he had been, who he was, and who he would be onward. From the little baby Brian to the adult man he had become, across the fields of teenage years, the small rivers marking the borders of the phases in his too short life, onto the pastures of adulthood, and sunsets at times of sorrow.

Across the fields of yesterday,
He sometimes comes to me
A little lad just back from play–
The lad I used to be.
And yet he smiles so wistfully
Once he has crept within,
I wonder if he hopes to see
The man I might have been.
    (Thomas S. Jones Jr, 1882–1932)

10
The 'Bribed Pathologist' and Other Nasties

A generous volume of accusations over the years has fallen against Dr Angus Sommerville, allegedly the bribed pathologist who performed Brian Jones' autopsy on 3 July 1969. It has been frequently suggested that he received a bribery in Dunlop shares on that day, to proceed on the autopsy post-haste, in order to manipulate autopsy findings. These claims and assumptions are based on Heward Dutchman & Co, Chartered Accountants in London, sending a letter to Dr Sommerville on 3 July 1969. The letter reads as follows:

> "Dear Dr Sommerville,
> I have pleasure acknowledging receipt of your letter you have received from your Stockbrokers relating to the purchase of your Dunlop shares. This gives me the information I require." – The letter ends with greetings and the sender's signature.

The wording may seem somewhat confusing, but it was probably logical in its original context. All the letter is saying is that Heward Dutchman & Co received a letter, or perhaps a copy of a letter, that Dr Sommerville had received from his Stockbrokers after his purchase of Dunlop shares. Logically, the Stockbrokers sent their letter to Dr Sommerville's place of residence. Dr Sommerville then informed his accountants Heward Dutchman & Co in London about this purchase, and the Chartered Accountants wrote to him to acknowledge the receipt of his letter. The order is that Dr Sommerville first made a purchase, Stockbrokers then confirmed it to him, after which Dr Sommerville wrote to notify his accountants, who then confirmed the receipt of his notification on 3 July 1969. All the above took some time with letters in transit after being typed out. There were no computers or fax machines; it happened by Royal Mail. There is nothing to suggest that Dr Sommerville received any Dunlop shares on 3 July 1969, and there is nothing to suggest bribery in any which way. The only thing that happened on 3 July 1969 was Heward Dutchman & Co confirming to Dr Sommerville in writing that they had received a letter from him, which had to be either before 3 July or on the very day. Be it either of the two, Brian Jones was very much alive at the time those shares were purchased by Dr Sommerville. Not that any of this matters anyway, because Dr Sommerville was not the pathologist performing the post mortem examination; he had nothing to do with it. Dr Angus Sommerville was the Coroner at the inquest on 7 July 1969.

The pathologist performing the autopsy was Dr Albert Sachs. The autopsy report specifically says that the autopsy, which is the same as a post-mortem examination, was performed by Dr Albert Sachs, and he signed the document. Dr Albert Sachs (1904-1976) was a highly distinguished pathologist born in Pretoria, South Africa, in 1904, and he graduated in medicine from Trinity College in Dublin in 1926. He joined the Royal Medical Corps in 1927 and was posted in India, where he excelled as a medical specialist. After WW2, Dr Sachs returned to the UK, and was appointed professor of pathology at the Royal Army Medical College in 1949. He retired from the Army after three years in this appointment in 1956, after which he was appointed consultant pathologist to the Queen Victoria Hospital, East Grinstead, Sussex. He was an enthusiastic and hard-working professional who published several papers in his specialist field. His colleagues at East Grinstead soon realized his competence and capabilities, and as one of them wrote, they "had acquired a man of rare character with immense charm and wide experience...who radiated good cheer which illuminated the lives of all who worked with him."[35] In short, he was a highly qualified and experienced pathologist in 1969, and there are no grounds to cast doubt on his professionalism. He performed a professional autopsy on Brian, and there was nothing he could possibly have gained from doing otherwise.

There is nothing peculiar about the time when the autopsy was performed. It is perfectly normal to do it within the first 24 hours, and leaving it for more than a few days would allow decomposition to begin, which may distort the condition of the organs as they were at the time of the person's passing. Then again, had the pathologist not done the autopsy as soon as he did, it would undoubtedly have raised claims that he intentionally delayed it, in order to allow decomposition to set in; damned if you do and damned if you don't. There is also no validity in claiming that bruises would have appeared on the skin, if Dr Sacs had delayed the autopsy, because that is obviously a preconceived assumption with no factual basis.

An internet myth of alleged bruises and a stab wound on Brian's body flourishes online, although there is no proof of any of that. But, as the story continues, there is no proof, because Dr Sachs was bribed. And, as you guessed, there is no proof he was bribed. The fallacy then continues that there is no proof, because the proof was hidden. Yet the absence of proof does not mean proof of absence, which in this context means that the absence of a record of bruising and a stab wound on the body is not proof of their existence hidden. That, in plain English, is rubbish. However, if new proof should emerge, it is fair to consider it reasonably and objectively, and accept its existence.

Equally, there is no validity in claiming that Dr Sachs ignored two spots on the skin: one allegedly yellow mixed with orange and the other purple. Yet there were no such spots on Brian's skin. The said spots do exist, but they are mentioned in the report prepared by Mr Cook, a biochemist in Royal Sussex Hospital in Brighton, and they were detected in tests made for the biochemical report on substances found in Brian's system. Those spots were detected with a method called 'Thin Layer Chromatography'. Chromatography is a laboratory technique used to separate chemical mixtures of substances into their components. The essence of the technique is that a mixture consisting of various substances is passed through another substance, e.g. filter paper. Different colour inks, turning the substances into different colours, allow the chemist to see particles travel at different speeds through the filter paper. A paper filter is only one of the options in chromatography, and thin layer chromatography has a different filtering method. But the principle remains the same. Thin layer chromatography is a subcategory of chromatography, and there is a lot of detailed information available on it online. Suffice to say, for our purposes, that during the analysis process different coloured spots arose on the laboratory platelets used, and that is what the spots referred to in connection with Brian's body are about. The spots were possibly due to diphenhydramine, which can be found together with methaqualone in Mandrax, and Brian is known to have taken Mandrax. But those spots were not on Brian's skin, and they were not bruises.

Another accusation thrown against details of the autopsy is that only certain substances were tested for. Yet the reality is that nobody will ever test for everything that may come to someone's mind, and the substances a body was typically tested for were opiates, benzoylecgonine, barbiturates, amphetamines, benzodiazepines, oxycodone and methadone.

Allegations continue that the pathologist must have been bribed, because the post-mortem report reads 'immersion in fresh water' towards the end of the report. It is alleged the report should read 'immersion in chlorinated water'. Yet what Dr Albert Sachs wrote in the report was exactly right: drowning was due to immersion in fresh water. An objective and reasonable person would read the report starting from the beginning, which is the way Dr Sachs performed the autopsy, making notes during it, and on conclusion he then wrote his report. If in doubt, check out episodes of *Silent Witness*, and while it is a TV-series and not real life, the method is logical. Dr Sachs started objectively with how the body was presented, and then proceeded with details about the inner organs. After he had examined everything, he drew a conclusion of what the examination showed as the cause of death. And because the way the organs manifested themselves in his examination, he concluded that the cause of death was drowning due to immersion in fresh water, and that is what the report says.

Drowning occurs when the respiratory tract is blocked by fluid. It may occur that there is not much water in the victim's lungs, because when water enters the windpipe, the body reacts with spasms of the larynx, commonly known as the voice box. Voice box contains the vocal cords, and we use it for breathing, swallowing and talking. The spasms are the body's automatic reaction to close the windpipe, to prevent more water from entering the lungs. From here onward, there is a difference between drowning in freshwater or saltwater.

When freshwater enters the lungs, the body absorbs the water through the walls of the veins into the blood stream, where it reduces the number of red blood cells, which results in lack of oxygen for the body, and a cardiac arrest occurs relatively quickly. Saltwater, on the other hand, has the opposite effect: the salt content causes water and blood from the bloodstream to cross from the capillary walls into the lungs. The heart beat slows down to sluggish, until a cardiac arrest occurs. The death occurs more slowly, and the physiological results are different in a post mortem report.

Chlorination of water is not a cause of death, so it does not matter whether the water was chlorinated or not. What mattered was that it was freshwater and not saltwater, and the conclusion is drawn by the pathologist on the victim's organs on the autopsy table. A pathologist does not make prior assumptions one way or another; he simply makes observations on the body before him.

As for the inquest on 7 July; it seems fair to say it was short, perhaps too short to be adequate. But there is no proof, at least so far, that the Coroner was bribed. If there were no police reports suggesting there may be something suspicious about the death of Brian Jones, the coroner, whose name and title were Dr Sommerville, had nothing before him to suggest Brian's drowning was anything other than a misadventure. He did not have anything else to go by. The pathologists report had no forensic evidence of a violent murder, and in the absence of any proof of a murder, the Coroner could objectively not conclude it was one. If Brian was pushed under water by his shoulders or his head, there would be no bruising arising. It is impossible to say what may have happened in that regard, and it seems very likely that he was pushed under water, but the Coroner proceeded on the documents before him on 7 July 1969. Neither did he mistake Brian's date of passing for 3 July 1969; the death certificate refers to the pathologist Dr Albert Sachs's autopsy report that records the time of death on 2 July, which is noted and passed on the registry of deaths by the coroner Dr Angus Sommerville. The tombstone was arranged by Brian's parents and it says what they wanted it to say, and whatever it says is no responsibility of an official of any kind.

Over the decades after 1969, many suggestions and theories have been presented for how it came about that Brian was killed in July 1969, and one of the frequent motives is that the other Stones wanted the Rolling Stones name after Brian was kicked out of his own group. Allegedly other Stones members fronted up at Cotchford, demanding the

Rolling Stones name from Brian, who had originally named the group he founded. But Brian did not register the name ever, nor could he have, because it was already registered to another group. He later modified the name to the Rolling Stones.

In 1965, Jones, Jagger, Richards, Wyman and Watts learnt about the name being registered to another group. The original group who named themselves The Rolling Stones had officially registered the name under the *Companies Act* in November 1957. It belonged to 3 brothers from Bristol, and they did some singing and performing at dances, although they were very different from the 5 Rolling Stones. The 5 Rolling Stones checked out the matter, and much to their surprise it was true. It was also written about in the *Daily Mail*, and as luck would have it, the person the reporter talked to was Brian Jones of the 3 Bristol Rolling Stones. They were all married and had a short hair; a totally different kettle of fish.[36]

However, the issue remains that in legal terms the remaining 4 Stones, with Mick Taylor already about to be added, could not ask Brian to grant them the group's name, because Brian did not own it, although, and as said before, it would have been difficult to force from Brian his right to continue to use the group name he had originally chosen. It would not have gone down well with the public either. Brian originally named his group *The Rollin' Stones* for the blues song titled *Rollin' stones* by an artist called Muddy Waters, a great blues idol of his, and the 5 Rolling Stones had been using the name through the 1960s and gained their fame under that group name. Also, in the absence of the legal owners of the name ever taking action about their name being used by the 5 Rolling Stones, it is possible that Brian intended to use the name later. It is also possible that when said he did not want to continue with the Stones music, he had already separated himself from the Rolling Stones name as well.

Another claim frequently mentioned is that Brian could not drown on his own, because he was a very good swimmer. And he was, to the extent that for a short time, before leaving Cheltenham for London, he worked as a lifeguard at the local swimming pool. He was confident and competent at swimming, and enjoyed swimming pools in Georgia and Florida on the Stones first 1965 American tour in May 1965. It was only about 4 years before he drowned, but in those 4 years he became a physically different man. His body deteriorated dramatically as discussed already, and he no longer kept physically active either. He was a far cry from the swimmer he was in May 1965. There is every reason to think he enjoyed swimming at Cotchford as well, but he was no longer the fit swimmer he was before. While it is theoretically possible that Brian perhaps fell unconscious and drowned on his own accord, which possibility remains for want of firm facts about how his drowning came about, it is highly likely that his swimming skills did not matter one way or another, because he was held under water, so that he drown.

Further stories abound about cuts on Brian's sides as a result of stabbing, but the post mortem report mentions none. Another thicket of stories are about Brian being given a shot of insulin, which would have made him unconscious and resulted in his drowning. Again, there is no proof for that, and while an insulin injection can make a non-diabetic unconscious, it does not happen every time. Obviously, if it does, an unconscious person drowns, when immersed in water, but there is no proof this happened with Brian. A further obstacle would be that syringes like the ones we have today for an insulin injection simply did not exist in the 1960s. Type 1 diabetes was mainly controlled with urine strips back then, and syringes available were two piece instruments, typically causing pain and infections in the injection area. It is unlikely to the umpteenth that Brian was surreptitiously injected by someone using a two-piece syringe. One-piece syringes became available in the 1970s.

Yet another claim has Brian stabbed in the house. Allegedly, he then fell and hit his head on the corner of a fireplace, and there remains a blood stain in place. After the stabbing, his body was rolled in a rug, taken in the pool, and Keylock burnt the rug on the bonfire. This claim only works in combination with a bribed pathologist, because the claim requires that Brian did not drown.

Another potential method toyed around with is that Brian was given an injection of insulin, which made him unconscious, after which he was held with his head down in a bucket of water. It is kind of an enhanced version of the first theory of insulin only. But this enhanced theory, as it were, fails because of the autopsy results: Brian died by drowning, which means that his lungs contained at least some water. If he was unconscious with his head held upside down in a bucket, he would not die of drowning but by lack of oxygen to the brain: if you drown with your head upside down, you must be conscious and struggle to breathe in air. It is not possible to be unconscious, have your head held upside down and breathe water into your lungs, yet Brian, irrefutably, died of drowning. And no, this was not covered up by a pathologist bribed with Dunlop shares: that did not happen.

11
What Was Brian Wearing?

What was Brian wearing when he drowned? It is such a superficially dumb question that the first reaction tends to be "well, whaddya think; he went for a swim in a swimming pool, so go and have a wild guess," after which you turn to anything else you were doing or thinking, huffing and puffing at such an intensely stupid question. But then, after a while or a few, a faint suspicion creeps inside with the suggestion that it might not be too bad an idea to reconsider those old perceptions firmly categorized in the pigeon holes of your mind.

The drowning of Brian Jones continues to be a dubious matter, and everything suggests it was not an accidental drowning. It is currently impossible to discuss the matter openly in books, because defamation law comes with its concerns, and one does not want to be squashed under an avalanche of ice and rocks from an alleged higher ground. Defamation law benefits the interests of those with unlimited finance to silence those with an unwelcome comment. It is the Western World's variant of censorship we hotly disapprove of in communist countries, past or present. Although it is self-evidently a means to control what other people say, and as such amounts to unfair tactics in legal terms, common sense says it is best to keep away from a landslide and not to get the stones rolling in the first place.

It is helpful, though, that many of those involved are already on pastures greener, and such concerns do not arise for those already there. Among them is Joan Fitzsimons, taxi driver, who died in 2002, and her lover Mushaser Yusef Ziyadch, deported to Jordan with date of death unknown. Central figures were Tom Keylock, employed by the Rolling Stones organization and Brian's minder until his drowning. He died on 2 July 2009, and two days later, on 4 July 2009, worldly life ended for Allen Klein, the Rolling Stones manager in the late 1960s. Builder Frank Thorogood died in 1993 and another builder John Betsworth in 1983. The third builder present at Cotchford was Maurice (Mo)Tucker, and he died in 2001. Janet Lawson, Keylock's lady friend, died in 2008, and Anna Wohlin, Brian's casual relationship at Cotchford, died in 2016-2017. Anita Pallenberg died in 2017, Nicholas Fitzgerald in 2009 and Suki Potier in 1981. The date of Mrs Hallet's death is not known. There is nothing to suggest that all these people had something to do with Brian's death, just that they are people who were present at Cothcford on 2 July 1969, and there may have been others, too.

But getting back to what Brian was wearing when he drowned: the witness statements of July 1969 in the matter validate the concern whether Brian Jones really went for a swim, because it is widely known that Anna Wohlin, Janet Lawson and Frank Thorogood all fabricated their witness statements. Not to mention that the first two also admitted doing that. Then decades later, Tom Keylock said that Wohlin and Lawson were deep in their narcotic oblivion after eating dope-laden hash cakes and a steak-and-kidney pie Thorogood had made.[37] It is reasonable to say that Brian had also enjoyed this fine cuisine from Thorogood's secret supplies. Those witness statements, wildly contradictory as if the witnesses all had failed the lying instructions they had been given, nonetheless did have in common that Thorogood went into the swimming pool to remove Brian's body. Things changed again years later, when Lawson told the newspaper *Mail on Sunday* in 2008 that she saw Frank do something to Brian. The remarkable difference is that while the witness statements of 1969, false as they were anyway, all said that Thorogood went in the water for Brian's body, Lawson changes the story dramatically in 2008 by saying that *Thorogood did something to Brian*. That means that Brian was still alive. There are two issues at play here: that Thorogood did something to Brian, and that Thorogood went to remove the body. They are two different instances, and between the first and the second Brian has passed away.

Lawson also made a comment about Wohlin not being much at Cotchford in the weeks leading up to the drowning incident, although she was not sure. Which would make sense in that Brian spent a fair bit of time in London in June, which, of course, is a wet rag in the face of those entertaining thoughts of Brian Jones and Anna Wohlin in the roles of the 20th century Romeo and Juliet. Fitzgerald also mentions that Wohlin only stayed the last two weeks at Cotchford, and the matter then becomes one of Lawson's definition of 'the weeks leading up to Brian's death'. She is, of course, no longer with us to elaborate further.

Nicholas Fitzgerald, staying in London at the time, wrote that he and his friend Richard Cadbury were present at

Cotchford on 2 July 1969. Fitzgerald said that Suki Potier had called him in London on 1 July and asked him to come down, because Brian was very distressed and fearful with what was happening at Cotchford. The following morning, 2 July, Fitzgerald received another phone call about Brian. This time the caller was a person called Ralph Hampton who lived near Hartsfield in Sussex. He had run into Brian outside the local pub the Hay Waggon the night before, and Brian had given him a pound and Fitzgerald's number. Brian had asked Hampton to call Fitzgerald with the request that Fitzgerald call Brian on the morning of 2 July, and keep calling until Brian himself would answer.

Fitzgerald, now concerned himself, decided to drive down with his friend Richard Cadbury and then call Brian from the Hay Waggon, where they were going to stop for lunch anyway. The two arrived in Hartfield around 1.30 pm, and then unexpectedly bumped into Brian at the pub. After a discussion at the Hay Waggon urinals, and before the threesome drove to Cotchford in Fitzgerald's car, Brian asked that Fitzgerald stay with him that night, to hold him. Brian was too scared to be on his own. On reaching Cotchford, Brian requested that Fitzgerald park the car further away, and they then arrived at the house on foot. Fitzgerald makes interesting comments about the three of them wondering why two spotlights were being installed above the swimming pool that afternoon.[38] It was the afternoon of the very day on which Brian would drown in the pool.

After spending some time with Brian, Fitzgerald and Cadbury left Cotchford, to return later around 11pm that night, as he and Brian had agreed earlier in the Hay Waggon around lunch time. But only the three of them knew about the plan. Upon arrival close by, Fitzgerald and Cadbury were blinded by the headlights of a foreign car: a vehicle with the driver's seat on the left-hand side was blocking the entry to the house. Was Allen Klein, the notorious Rolling Stones manager from the US, in attendance? Did he arrive at Cotchford unannounced after most of the attendees had left, leaving Brian alone with those who had a bone to pick with him? Did he and Keylock arrive there unannounced?

They must have, because photos taken at Brian's funeral on 10 July show Keylock holding his arm around heart-broken Suki Potier. Considering that only false witness statements were heard at the inquest on 7 July, Suki was blissfully ignorant of Keylock's presence at Cotchford at the time of Brian's murder. So, Klein and Keylock arrived later. And Suki was supported at the funeral by a wolf in sheep's clothing.

Forty years later, in 2009, Keylock admitted that he was at Cotchford on 2 July, and he said there were still some people whose names had not been mentioned regarding that night. With Klein and Keylock arriving unannounced later, the horror Brian would have felt in the last hour of his life must have been indescribable. Klein was an aggressive businessman who wanted things his way, undoubtedly thinking that when he walked past you, you were blinded by the halo surrounding his derrière. He would want to drive in the way he was accustomed to, and that was in a left-hand drive in America.

He was definitely in London in early July, as well as in contact with the Stones in person. Perhaps he was staying at the Londonderry House Hotel where the Stones and their entourage were apparently staying and where they had their meeting place for their Hyde Park concert on 5 July. On 4 July, the Stones had a practice session for the concert at the Beatles Apple studios, after which they returned to the hotel.[39] This means that they were at the hotel already. The preparations for the concert had taken weeks at least, and Brian's replacement Mick Taylor was going to be introduced. For all this to be happening, the group manager had to be involved. Klein was also photographed attending the Hyde Park concert two days later, 5 July 1969. The concert began at 1pm, and the Stones were the last performers after 6 others before them. But since Klein was the manager and participating in the arrangements, it is naïve to think he left his arrival till the last minute. In particular, in his capacity as 'chief of security' for the Stones, he had to be there days before to plan ahead what was required for the security.[40]

A theoretical but most unlikely scenario is available under Pan Am Airlines operations in 1969. Pan Am airlines ran a 'Round-the-world' schedule starting from New York, with a stop-over in London, Frankfurt, Istanbul, Beirut, Tehran, New Delhi, Bangkok, Hong Kong, Tokyo and Honolulu, after which the flight ended in Los Angeles for maintenance. Departures from New York were on Monday, Wednesday and Friday at 8 pm and arrival at Los Angeles at 8pm two days later, i.e. on the third day. Departing from New York on this flight, which was the quickest connection and there were many others available, would have you arrive in London at 7.40 am a day later: e.g. you fly out on Monday night and you arrive in London on Wednesday morning. Flying across five time zones would cause a jet lag, and time would be needed to recover. For Klein to attend at Hyde Park on 5 July, he had to leave no later than Wednesday, to arrive in London on

Friday morning. The likelihood of that being Klein's arrival schedule is very remote indeed. Whatever it was, Allen Klein was definitely in England when Brian Jones was killed.

Going back to the foreign vehicle with the driver's seat on the left at Cotchford late on 2 July 1969: we do not know the plates of the vehicle, but it was also easy and convenient to fly e.g. to Frankfurt, hire a vehicle there and drive it across. Indeed, there is no proof for this scenario, but the proven facts are that Klein was in London Town and that he was in the company of the Stones during the week of Brian's death, murder as it seems to be. Or perhaps Klein kept a regular vehicle for himself in England, because he had a lot of business there? The description of the vehicle Fitzgerald saw matches the scenario, and it all makes sense. It is fair to consider it likely that the Stones know where Klein was on 2 and 3 July 1969, and they remain probably the only ones left to cast light on the matter. It may be they would deny any knowledge regarding the matter, but everyone is free to believe it or not, because opinions are permitted.

Fitzgerald writes that Cadbury and him arrived at Cotchford around 11.15 pm. The drive to the house ran off Cotchford Lane. As they came into the lane, they were blinded with two powerful headlights on high beam glaring into their windshield from a fixed position; was that Keylock's car? After that, setting off toward the headlights about fifty yards away, they found a foreign car, left-hand drive, blocking the drive to the house itself; the car Klein drove? The driver's door was open, but there was no driver or passengers. Fitzgerald and Cadbury then walked around the hedges and trees to the side of the house, behind the small summer house close to the pool, where they remained hiding. The floodlights that were installed in the afternoon were now on, and the place was well lit with light streaming out from the windows of the building. Fitzgerald and Cadbury had a clear view of the pool, and they saw three men, dressed in sweaters and jeans, standing at the far-right corner of the swimming pool. Their clothes suggested they were workmen. But the power of the spotlights blotted out their features and made their faces look like white blobs, so Fitzgerald could not recognize them.

The moment Fitzgerald became aware of them, the one in the middle dropped to his knees and reached into the water, to push down on top of a head that looked white. At the opposite side, on far left, there was a man and a woman gazing down in the pool, while the man kneeling down was pushing down on the head, to keep it under water. Then the man to the right of the kneeling man said what sounded like a command, but all Fitzgerald could hear was '...do something'. Immediately the third man jumped into the water, arms outstretched and knees bent, and landed on the back of the person struggling in the water. The man who made the command to do something seemed about to jump in as well.

Fitzgerald and Cadbury were horrified at the scene. The woman on the left was slightly in the shadow so they could not see her face either. Shocked and horrified, Fitzgerald and Cadbury were wondering why she and the man did not make a move to help the person in the pool. They were considering doing something themselves, when suddenly out of the bushes next to them burst out a brawny man wearing spectacles. He pushed Cadbury aside and grabbed Fitzgerald's shoulder, and put his fist menacingly in his face. He snarled in his Cockney accent: "Get the hell out of here, Fitzgerald, or you'll be the next."[41]

That man fits the description of Tom Keylock, and before passing away in July 2009, he admitted that both himself and Fitzgerald were present on that night. Fitzgerald said he heard the voice on another occasion, and that was at the Hyde Park concert on 5 July, when he was standing on the side of the stage. Fitzgerald recognized the voice as the voice he had heard 3 days earlier at Cotchford. The man was commenting on how stupid it was to have butterflies released at the concert, and Fitzgerald's description of what the man was wearing matches the clothes Keylock was wearing in photos taken on the day, which was a red jacket and white trousers. Fitzgerald still did not know his name, and he quickly made another hasty exit to get away from the voice.[42]

It is difficult to establish who the woman standing by the pool may have been, although a guess comes to mind. But there was also the fourth man, and there is every reason to believe he was Klein. That there were 3 builders present does not mean that the 3 were standing together on one side of the pool; the order could have been anything. The fourth man was not Keylock, because Keylock was an extra who suddenly stepped out of the bushes to frighten off Fitzgerald and Cadbury, for which reason Keylock was present but he did not physically kill Brian, unless matters changed after Fitzgerald and Cadbury ran for their lives to get out of Cotchford.

By then, Fitzgerald and Cadbury were shaking with fear, and once him and Cadbury got back to their car, they revved up the engine, reversing into the main road, and their tyres were screeching. The noise they made was enough to wake up the whole village, but the two were wanting to get the away in horror, so much so that they were going in the opposite direction toward Uckfield instead of London. It did not matter where they were travelling, as long as it was away from Cothcford and those who murdered Brian.[43]

Mrs Hallett, Brian's housekeeper, talks about cars screeching away from Cotchford at a time she described as 'dusk was approaching', which, admittedly, is a vague expression. Sunset in southern England on 2 July is at 9.20pm, but it can take 50 minutes before it gets dark, so it seems Mrs Hallett was referring to the time around 10.30–11pm, when the sun has already gone down but total darkness has not fallen yet. According to Les Hallet, her husband, there was shouting and roaring of car engines, and it appears to fit in with what Fitzgerald described as his hasty retreat from Cotchford.[44]

Joan Fitzsimons was the lady friend of Frank Thorogood, the builder in charge of Cotchford repair works in 1969. She had two boyfriends simultaneously in 1969, and Brian knew them both. They were also both present at Cotchford on 2 July.. Thorogood was much older than the younger boyfriend Mushaser Yusef Ziyadch, aged 19 back then and born in Jordan. Fitzsimons continued to see Thorogood while seeing Ziyadch at the same time, and Thorogood was aware of Ziyadch's physical prowess over him, which would leave him as a runner-up, if male physical prowess was what Fitzsimons entertaining the company of either was seeking. Thorogood felt deeply humiliated by the two, especially before Brian at Cotchford, because Brian would typically laugh at the on-going tragic trilogy with no winners in sight.

Ziyadch had been all day at Cotchford, while Fitzsimons had been out working. She came to pick him up at 9pm, and they both left. Talking about the night in 2009, Ziyadch said to the effect that there were many people present, with Brian and Thorogood in argument when he left. All those present have passed away. Of those 12-13 present Thorogood, Keylock, Allen Klein, Morris (Mo) Tucker and John Betsworth had business matters to settle with Brian. Thorogood was particularly incensed with Brian, who had poked fun out of his balding head and the triangle tragedy in his love life. And there were hash cakes and marijuana-spiced steak and kidney pie, all to be washed down with a generous amount of drinks with alcoholic content, and feelings were running hot and high.

But, notably, over all the years and across all statements interviews and comments, nobody ever said it was a pool party; pool parties were not held in those days in England, and not extensively these days either. It could not have been one, because it all happened in the afternoon and late evening, so you could not enjoy the sun while chatting to others, and there were no pool games like water polo. Rather, it was a booze-and-pie to sort out business matters, and for Brian to get rid of Thorogood with his workers, including telling Wohlin to pack her bags as well. The air temperature had been dropping steadily since 12 noon, when it may have been hot around a good 30°C, and the cooler air rolling in required warmer clothing; trousers, shoes, tops and perhaps a jacket or a sweater. Nobody was prancing around in their bathers, and no comment has been made that anyone did on that day. By the time arguments got very hot, not that they were pleasant at any time of the day, it was getting increasingly dark, and the sunset was at 9.20pm. Against that background, it certainly seems that Brian did not go swimming late at night; why would he? Why would he get into his bathers on a cold night, when he was having a major disagreement with four or five fully clothed aggressive men against him?

Brian was tragically outnumbered against those four or five men, who were Thorogood, Tucker, Betsworth, Keylock and apparently Klein, and he was on his own against them. That Brian ended up in the pool can only be the result of someone pushing him in, or he fell. It is likely he was pushed in, like he pushed in Thorogood earlier in June, when he was poking fun out of Thorogood's demise as a discarded lover. But it could have been any other of the men pushing him in, either intentionally or accidentally, and betting on intentional seems a good choice, because Brian had finished his business matters with the builders by telling them he was not going to pay more, which did not please them any better than Brian's plans for a new group with Lennon or anybody else would have pleased Klein. Perhaps the situation was out of control, but it is more likely it was progressing in the way planned.

When Brian fell in the pool, he must have been fully clothed, in all likelihood wearing trousers, shoes, a top and something warmer for his upper body. He had had alcohol like all others, as well as some tablets. It may be this is the situation that Fitzgerald spotted from amongst the bushes, when he said he saw three men on one side and another man with a woman staring at a figure floating in the pool. That would mean that Brian was still alive; he would sink, when his lungs filled up with water and air escaped from his clothes. But if Brian was wearing suitable clothing for the time of the day and he had alcohol and hash cakes in his system, he would have had extreme difficulty to swim. It is not easy to swim with all those clothes on, and if he was pushed in, he had no time to prepare and was taken by a surprise. Given all that, it was easy for someone to push him down for him to drown. The woman Fitzgerald saw was not mentioned in any of the witness statements made, but considering that those present contradicted themselves and each other over the years, it is impossible to say who she was. It is possible it was Lawson, whom Fitzgerald and Cadbury spotted from their twiggy hideaway. Or it could have been a woman with Klein. Lawson later said it was her, although she also said earlier she could not have been it, because she had eaten hash cakes. It seems Wohlin was somewhere around as well, that somewhere probably being an upstairs bedroom where she lay zonked out. The witness statements are conflicting, but they all place Thorogood in the pool removing Brian's body. There is no way Wohlin, a very slim young woman, would have been able to do it.

Interestingly, Lawson commented in 2008 that with Brian at the bottom of the pool, there was steam coming up from the water. For the water to produce steam, there had to be warm water and cold air. Wohlin said that Brian kept the water temperature at 30°C (86°F), because she liked to swim in warm water. Presumably she was reliable enough for that piece of information, although not much else, but her claim about the water temperature seems to be proven by Lawson's later comment that there was steam rising from the water. The steam developed as a result of the major temperature difference between the cold late night air and the pool's warmer water: cold and dry air moving over warm, moist pool water forces some of the water to evaporate. But that steam was emerging from the water confirms that air was much colder, for which reason nobody was running around barefoot in swim wear. Further, Lawson saying that Frank lifted Brian from the bottom of the pool, does not exclude the likelihood that others were involved, and that would be 'the other at least 3 men by the pool', as Fitzgerald said. It is possible Thorogood was not the only one who get wet, on top of Brian being soaked through already.

We do not know how Tucker and Betsworth came to disappear from Cotchford, yet they were gone by the morning. But it is easy to imagine that after Brian was pulled out, his clothes were removed and he was re-dressed in wet bathers; we do not know, because nothing has been said of what Brian was wearing on the paramedics' arrival on 3 July. What we do know is that Keylock appears in an impeccably ironed white shirt and impeccably pressed trousers before journalists on 3 July, which seems odd, unless he had a reason to change into fresh clothing he brought along the day before. It is likely that what he was wearing on 2 July got wet, and whatever else got wet in the process of Brian Jones being killed, including Brian's or anyone else's wet clothes, was burnt in the bonfire Keylock lit before the police arrived on 3 July. And that would explain the need for the peculiar bonfire, because it was not lit without a reason.

It also seems that Thorogood was framed posthumously for killing Brian, because he was the first of the main characters to move onto pastures greener. Keylock said he visited terminally ill Thorogood in November 1993. Keylock alleged that during the visit Thorogood confessed to killing Brian, and then conveniently died before he could elaborate further. With builder John Betsworth passing away around 1983 and Mo Tucker in 2001, Keylock himself still had his own interests to protect, as well as those of Allen Klein. It most certainly seems that Klein was there when Brian was killed. There is nothing to suggest that other Stones members went anywhere near Cotchford on 2 July, but Klein, while looking after his own business interests, was also looking after the interests of the Stones; he was their manager. Of course, Keylock would not implicate Klein in any which way during his life time. When Keylock died on 2 July 2009, Klein was still alive, if only another 2 days, and he died on 4 July 2009.

12
Hyde Park 5 July 1969

The first week of July 1969 was hot and humid in southern England. It was the time of high summer with heady fragrance from blooming bushes infiltrating the air as best it could, although where it failed and remained on too low a level, it caused hay fever, headaches and asthma attacks. Families and friends of every local Hyacinth Bucket were enjoying cucumber sandwiches and chicken vol-au-vents with shandy in the hydrangea gardens of leafy suburbs that offered motley shade for nesting birds. Evenings were sultry with stagnant air, to the discontent of most, although married couples in bad relationships, for whom hot weather offered a plausible excuse to put off semi-obligatory relations neither wished for, felt a welcome relief to continue their pretence for yet another night.

In London Proper the heat persisted throughout the week, and those who ventured downtown, enjoyed every shady spot, water fountain and lake in the parks. Tens of thousands of young adults and hippies headed to Hyde Park for the free Rolling Stones concert on 5 July, and as they walked along the footpaths and drenched their thirst with beer and Coke, a state of shock and confusion from Brian Jones death was riding in the air like an invisible pestilence, trickling down from tree tops to plants, leaves and dry grass, where it mixed with humidity and then vapourised as the disbelief everyone felt.

The news about Brian Jones death had spread since Wednesday, when it was first reported, but the two days before the concert had allowed the news to reach everyone who wanted to know. The shining musician and visual attraction of the Rolling Stones was gone. The musically minded were feeling the loss of a rare talent impossible to replace, and women who had been hoping for carnal passion with Brian were licking their wounds caused by the loss of a future opportunity. The first week without Brian was intense with awe and sorrow, which made people feel as uncomfortable as the humid heat they could not escape.

Perhaps people who attended in Hyde Park found what they were looking for, although musical satisfaction was likely to remain absent with those on stage performing poorly. The first week without Brian Jones brought the realization of death and closure to the younger generation who only knew a future seemingly with no end. Suddenly they saw how quickly and seemingly senselessly night can fall, and the door that had closed with no prior warning left confusion and sorrow in the hearts of those left behind. The golden Brian Jones era had ended, but many unanswered questions remained with more disbelief arising in the years to come about the way Brian had been killed.

Whether it was the end of his life is a matter of perception, and may those with opposing or differing views hold onto their own. But Ovid, the author of the expansive opus *Metamorphoses*, written in Latin ca. 800 CE, held that:

"All things are changing; nothing dies. The spirit wanders, comes now here, now there, and occupies whatever frame it pleases… For that which once existed is no more, and that which has not come to be; and so the whole round of motion is gone through again."

While Brian himself was not ready to leave this world behind, he had forebodings in the shape of fears he held. He knew intuitively things were revolving around him at an ever-increasing pace out of his control, and he was wary like on animal relying on its instincts. He anticipated destruction, but could not see its shape and form. Sadly, his instincts were right, and his life came to an ugly end. But that will not decimate the validity of who he was and the legacy he left behind.

Brian had great insight into life, and he was perceptive of life's deeper meaning in various connections. He disclosed some of his views on life in an interview published in *Disc and Music Echo* magazine on 21 January 1967:

"I'm learning about a lot of weird things. I feel it's necessary because I was thrown at a very tender and immature age into a world I knew little about …

It's not a question of beliefs – it goes much further than that. I have certain devotions in a way, but I don't have enough knowledge to talk about them.

I have a code by which I lead my life and I'm trying to develop this: Before one makes any sort of statement or proclamation about one's personal beliefs I think one must have the knowledge… I don't feel the time is right for me to say. One day, maybe, I feel that I have to say something, but not at this moment".

In celebration of all things bright and beautiful about Brian Jones and his life, what better way to conclude than with a poem called *Short Measures* by Ben Jonson (1572–1637). It is not the number of years but what those years may entail. What is necessary in life need not be provided in a multitude of decades; a much shorter period of time may suffice instead. If you already understand to see with your heart, you no longer need lessons in the tutelage of Athena, the Greek goddess of wisdom, reason, craft, civilization and justice. Remember, pure joy is always a matter of serendipity, so beware: it may happen to you anytime, and when it does, you will glow like a golden lantern on a dark winter's night.

> It is not growing like a tree
> In bulk, doth make man better be;
> Or standing long an oak, three hundred year,
> To fall a log at last, dry, bald and sere:
> A lily of a day
> Is fairer far in May,
> Although it fall and die that night
> It was the plant and flower of light.
> In small proportions we just beauties see;
> And in short measures life may perfect be.

May Brian Jones be enjoying a contented heart where his travels have taken him.

Annexures

Brian Jones' 'Brave New World'; newspaper clipping

Nansladron; newspaper clipping

'The economy is a joke'; newspaper clipping

Post-mortem report by Dr Sachs

London accountants' letter to Dr Somerville, Coroner

Pathology report

Death Certificate

Tom Keylock and Nicholas Fitzgerald (?) at Hyde Park

Nicholas Fitzgerald

Rolling Stones manager Allen Klein at Hyde Park

BRIAN JONES'S BRAVE NEW WORLD:
"My world would be a world without sickness ... a world where sickness of the body and of the mind would cease to exist. I'd like lots of money spent on neuro-research, to find out what causes mental illness. When man can understand the human brain he'll understand everything. A world without sickness would be a world without cruelty, and that's everything."

N.B. Every effort has been made to trace copyright holders, but any who may have been overlooked are invited to contact the publisher.

ornamented belt.

"I want to buy the farm so that I can become completely self-sufficient. I think the British economy is in danger of collapse, so I want to be able to grow all my own food and be completely independent of everyone . . . it's in Southern Cornwall, near the coast. There's some good shark fishing there. I've caught one myself, a 25 pounder.

"I shall keep Friesian cattle, pigs and poultry and have my own farm manager, and I shall spend most of my time there. It's only five hours from London by road so I shall just come up when I need to and stay overnight. And I love all this electronic music, and African music. I was on holiday in Marrakesh, and there was a festival of music there, all different sorts of music. I put it all down on tape.

BRIAN JONES

'The economy is a joke'

"THE NEW single, 'Jumpin' Jack Flash', has a basic guitar riff pattern. That's why it will get compared to 'Satisfaction', but I don't think it is a reversal at all."

Brian, who says he cringes when he looks down the charts and sees Tom Jones, Engelbert Humperdinck and Des O'Connor, is buying a farm in Devon, as is Keith.

"The economy is a joke nowadays. I must be self sufficient and able to do without money. It is so peaceful down there with the sea so close.

"It is such a paradoxical situation. Here I am, hung up on electronic music, London and the pop scene, and there I want to go and live in the country. I guess I would become a commuter.

"Getting a single in the charts has never really bothered me. I have always been more keen to see our albums selling well, but as 'Jumpin' Jack Flash' marks our first release for a while, I would like to see it right at the top.

"It is, as I have said, a basic riff pattern, and for that reason I thought it might come in for some heavy criticism from the record reviewers. You know, going on about retrogression and going commercial again.

"But on the contrary, it got some great reviews, and lots of people have said it is just what is needed to put some good basic excitement back in the charts."

Notes of the Post-Mortem Examination of

Name of deceased	Lewis Brian Jones.
Age	26
Sex	Male
Address of deceased	Cotchford Farm, Hartfield, Sussex.
Name of G.P.	
Observers present at examination	C.I.D.
Date and time of examination	Mortuary, Queen Victoria Hospital,
Place where examination performed	E. Grinstead, 3rd July, 1969.
Estimated time of death	11.30 - midnight 2nd July, 1969.

If a histological or bacteriological examination is to be made the pathologist will initial here:

Chief points in the history of the case.	Deceased apparently went for a swim in a pool at his home with friends. Friends left the pool and the deceased decided to stay in the water. Last seen alive 11.30 p.m. 2nd July, 1969. Found dead shortly afterwards.
EXTERNAL EXAMINATION Height(length), Weight	5' 9".
Apparent age	26 years of age.
Nourishment	Powerfully built, with a tendency to obesity.
Temperature at rectum	Not taken.
Rigor mortis, hypostasis, decomposition	Rigor mortis present. Hypostasis present.
Evidence of violence, burns	Nil.
Identification (tattoo marks, old scars, special deformities	Nil seen.
Body surface - Pallor abnormal coloration	Pallor of face. Frothy fluid round nostrils.
Orifices of body, hair, teeth	Own teeth.
INTERNAL EXAMINATION Cranial Cavity Skull, scalp and face	N.A.D.
Brain - weight, etc.	Wt. 1553gms. Congested and oedematous. Punctate haemorrhages in white matter.
Meninges and blood vessels	Congested.
Spinal column, cord and meninges	N.A.D.
Thoracic Cavity Mouth, tongue, tonsils, oesophagus	Little blood stained fluid in mouth. Could be due to artificial respiration.
Larynx, trachea, bronchi, thyroid and thymus glands	Respiratory tract. Mucosa congested. Bronchi contains a few flakes of glairy mucus, but this is not the viscid adherent mucus associated with death due to an asthmatic attack.
Lungs, pleurae, diaphragm	Wt. L 632gms, R 643gms. Adhesions left base to chest wall. No free fluid to pleural cavities. Both lungs voluminous. Some areas of collapse. Lungs
Pericardium	pit on pressure. Frothy blood stained fluid exudes from lungs on section. Few subpleural petechial
Heart (size, weight, cavities and contents valve orifices and valves), heart muscle and coronary arteries	haemorrhages. Heart Wt. 411gms. General hypertrophy. Both sides dilated. Myocardium fatty and flabby. No evidence of vascular or valvular disease.

EAST SUSSEX RECORD OFFICE

Aorta, pulmonary and other blood vessels	Blood from left side of heart showed 29% Hb plasma due to haemolysis. Aorta. Narrow but no... Blood alcohol 140 mgs %
Internal injuries (thoracic)	Nil.
Abdominal Cavity Stomach and contents	About 1oz. of undigested food in fluid. Mucosa congested.
Peritoneum, intestines and contents, appendix, mesenteric glands, etc.	N.A.D.
Liver and gall bladder	Wt. 3000gms. Congested. Architecture lost. Sections show liver dysfunction due to extensive fatty degeneration. Gall bladder. Empty.
Spleen	Spleen Wt. 247gms. Congested.
Kidneys and ureters	Wt. L 190gms. R 181gms. Congested.
Bladder and urine	Little urine present. Analysis showed 1720 micrograms. % of a basic amphetamine-like substance.
Suprarenals, pancreas	Apparently normal.
Generative organs, breasts, prostate, etc.	Normal for age.
Internal injuries (abdominal)	Nil.
Are all other organs healthy?	Apparently.

Cause of death as shown by the examination :	In my opinion the cause of death was :-
I Disease or condition directly leading to death * ... ... Antecedent causes ... ... Morbid conditions, if any, giving rise to the above cause stating the underlying condition last ...	I (a) Drowning. due to (or as a consequence of) (b) Immersion in fresh water. due to (or as a consequence of) (c)
II Other significant conditions, contributing to the death, but not related to the disease or condition causing it ≠	II Severe liver dysfunction due to fatty degeneration and the ingestion of alcohol and drugs.

* This does not mean the mode of dying, such as, e.g. heart failure, asphyxia, asthenia, etc., it means the disease, injury or complication which caused death.

≠ Conditions which do not in the pathologist's opinion contribute materially to the death should not be included under this heading

These notes should be short and concise records of the facts observed; if opinions are expressed the grounds upon which they are based should also be stated. Scientific terms should be avoided when possible.

Any further remarks : In death from an asthmatic attack lungs are light and bulky.

Signature and qualifications Albert Sachs, CB, CBE, MD, MSc, FRCP, F, C ,Path
Address   Queen Victoria Hospital. E. Grinstead, Sussex.

Date 6th July, 1969

HEWARD DUTCHMAN & CO
CHARTERED ACCOUNTANTS

F.C. ROSSITER, F.C.A.

TELEPHONE 01-606 7510 & 7551

CROSS KEYS HOUSE,
56, MOORGATE,
LONDON, E.C.2.

FCR/SMD

3rd July, 1969.

Dr. A. C. Sommerville,
Beckford,
East Grinstead,
Sussex.

Dear Dr. Sommerville,

I have pleasure in acknowledging receipt of your letter you have received from your Stockbrokers relating to the purchase of your Dunlop shares. This gives me the information I require.

Yours sincerely,

UNBRIDGE WELLS GROUP HOSPITAL MANAGEMENT COMMITTEE
THE QUEEN VICTORIA HOSPITAL
EAST GRINSTEAD, SUSSEX

PATRON
H.M. QUEEN ELIZABETH, THE QUEEN MOTHER

HONORARY PRESIDENT
GLADYS, LADY KINDERSLEY

PATHOLOGICAL LABORATORY   7th July, 1969.

FRCP. F.C. Path.

Telephone report from Mr. Cook, Biochemist, Royal Sussex Hospital, Brighton.

1. **Blood barbiturate.**   Nil.

2. **Blood alcohol.**   140mgs) (Approx 7 whiskeys, or 3½ pints of beer)

3. **Urine.**   Amphetamine like substance 1720 micro-gms. (in normal urine this never exceeds 200 micro gms.) These figures suggest ingestion of a fairly large quantity of a drug

4. **Thin layer chromatography.**   Failed to reveal the presence of the following in an unchanged state.
    (a) Amphetamine.
    (b) Methedrine.
    (c) Morphine.
    (d) Methadrone.
    (e) Isoprenaline.

But did show the presence of 2 dense spots, one reddish orange which has not been identified and the other a purple spot. This could be due to diphenhydramine, which is present together with methaqualone in Mandrax, which the deceased is known to have taken.

CERTIFIED COPY **OF AN ENTRY**
Pursuant to the Births and Deaths Registration Act 1953

DEATH

Entry Number: 108

Registration District: Uckfield
Sub-district: East Grinstead
Administrative area: County of East Sussex

1. Date and place of death: Second July 1969, Cotchford Farm, Hartfield
2. Name and surname: Lewis Brian JONES
3. Sex: Male
4. Maiden surname of woman who has married: —
5. Date and place of birth: 28th February 1942, Cheltenham Glos.
6. Occupation and usual address: Entertainer, Cotchford Farm Hartfield
7. (a) Name and surname of informant: Certificate received from A.C. Sommerville, Coroner for East Sussex. Inquest held 7th July 1969
   (b) Qualification:
   (c) Usual address: —
8. Cause of death:
   I a browning
   b Immersion in Fresh Water
   II Severe liver dysfunction due to fatty degeneration and the ingestion of alcohol and drugs. Swimming whilst under the influence of alcohol and drugs. MISADVENTURE
9. I certify that the particulars given by me above are true to the best of my knowledge and belief.
   Signature of informant: —
10. Date of registration: Ninth July 1969
11. Signature of registrar: M.P. Lacey Registrar

Certified to be a true copy of an entry in a register in my custody.
J Purcell   Deputy Superintendent Registrar   10th July 1992

Tom Keylock, dressed in white trousers and a red jacket, is opening boxes of white butterflies on the side of the stage at the Hyde Park concert on 5 July 1969.

It would appear behind him is Nicholas Fitzgerald, because the scene is exactly as Fitzgerald described it in his book and the image had not appeared on YouTube in 1969. Fitzgerald could be either of the two men marked with a white arrow.

Nicholas Fitzgerald in the early 1980s, without a moustache.

Two images of Allen Klein, sitting on the side of the stage at the Hyde Park concert on 5 July 1969.

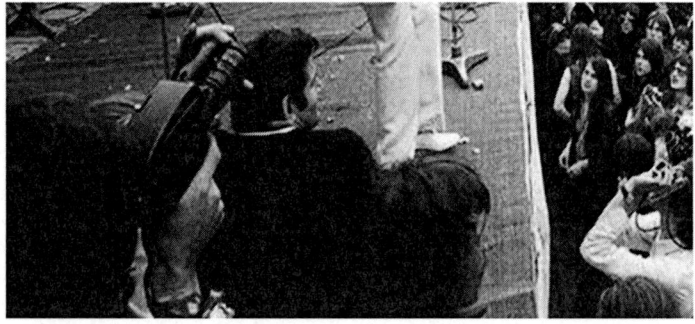

English translation of the German article on Brian Jones in *BRAVO* in June 1969

Brian Jones is leaving the Stones! When I heard this piece of news, I could not believe it. On the way to London on a plane, I had only one thought: it cannot be true. In the last years, I went through many crises with the Rolling Stones, but the Rolling Stones continued to roll every time. No denying that Brian only got more difficult in recent times, and the differences between him and the group only greater. But splitting up? Can there be Rolling Stones without Brian Jones?

Soon after arrival in London I am already all pessimistic, despite the bright sunshine outside. As I am climbing up the stairs to the Stones Head Office at 46 Maddox Street, Keith Richards races by me hurdling over the steps. Am I seeing ghosts? A Rolling Stones on an afternoon at 2.30pm?

"Hi Thomas', the ghost greets me. 'I'm in a hurry. See you later'! I ran upstairs after him to the office, where Mick, Charlie and Bill are sitting. Brian is not there. Four Stones throw an embarrassed smile at me and nobody says anything."

I brought along BRAVO issue no 25 with me, and show them the full colour middle page to the Stones. 'In this article, I made the announcement that you are planning a tour in Germany in the coming autumn. Will Brian be coming along'? – Mick shakes his head and says 'no' in a very determined tone of voice. "It is final: we and Brian have split up." – I look at Bill and Charlie, as if asking them for their opinion. They both nod, and Bill adds 'as friends'.

Really? As friends? Without any disagreement? C'mon, I know 'my 'Stones! But before I have a chance to ask more questions, the Stones chauffeur appears and the four disappear in a matter of seconds. – "I'll see you later, Thomas," shouts Mick to me on his way down the stairs.

I leaf through the newspapers lying on the table, and notice a sentence "Brian Jones flew to Africa on holiday, to make up his mind about his future without being disturbed." – Well that cannot be true, I think, and insist on Tom Keylock telling me, if it is true. He admits that Brian is staying with a friend in London. Tom relents to give me a phone number, and after the phone rings a couple of times, Brian picks up the phone. "I do not give any interviews," growls Brian in a sleepy voice. "I have said all I have to say, and it is all in the newspapers." – Yup, I say, but it also says in the papers that you are in Africa. "Okay okay," Brian softens up. "Come back in three weeks. I will not speak to any journos before that."– "Not even with an old friend," I ask. The line goes quiet, and I think he'll hang up soon. – "Put me on to Tom," Brian says. – Tome picks up the phone, listens for a while, says okay, and hangs up. "I've been asked to take you to Brian tonight," he says to me, "but keep it to yourself!"

Hours later, on way through dark London, I think back on the previous 7 years. It was exactly 7 years ago when Brian played with his 3-man group on stage of a shabby pub in Ealing his hot music. Two guys jumped on stage to him—I met the Stones in the previous 4 years many times, and Brian was my favourite. He may well be the most difficult of the five guys, the most sensitive and hard at the same time. But always a good friend.

And here is he sitting opposite me in his secret hide-away. He has grown a beard. "So you want to hear the truth from me," he says, in an ironic tone of voice. "Well then, the old

Stones sound is not what I like anymore. I think it is a thing of the past. I would like to write and play my own music. After friendly discussions, we came to the conclusion that separation is the only solution there is. Happy with that?" – I asked "is there really no way that you will get together again?" – "No way whatsoever," replied Brian. "I wanted to leave over two years ago, but Mick convinced me to stay. But there is no going back anymore."

I watch Brian topping up his glass of whisky. He looks pale, exhausted and unwell, and not at all happy. I encourage him with "you know, the Stones are planning to go on tour again. I think the fans will miss you." – "You think so? Brian's face brightens up. 'Tell them that I will soon be back with my own group. It will be decided on in the next few weeks. Perhaps I will only produce music. One thing I know for sure: I would like to become rich, finally lay my hands on big money, like Mick and Keith…"

Brian jumps up, rummages through his box of records, and throws an LP at me. *JouJouka*, says the cover. – "I produced that in Algeria; my first LP. Would you like to hear it," asks Brian.

Of course I do. The next 20 minutes I spend listening to flutes and dogs barking. "It is genuine African folk music," says Brian. "Recorded in the streets in the middle of the night." He is very excited about the music, but I am not. – "This is music," delights Brian. "I will be composing in this style."

Depressed, almost shattered, I leave Brian. I fear it will take a long time before Brian, the lost Stone, will be a rich man. The next evening I drive to Olympic Studios, where the Stones are recording their new single *Honky Tonk Woman*…

Mick asks: "did you talk to him? In that case he probably told you we will continue to be friends. Keith, Bill, Charlie and I say so, too."

Whether it was separation as friends or foes unimportant to the Stones fans in the end. ... I ask "Are you not afraid that news about Brian could damage the Stones reputation?" – Mick replies with "I think our bad reputation has improved lately, and we are even without Brian far from finished."

Bibliography

Adams F, *The Genuine Works of Hippocrates.* The Sydenham Society, London (1849).

BRAVO magazine article, 16 June 1969.

British Medical Journal, 1976.

Brod, Max, *Franz Kafka: A Biography*, Schocken Books, NY (1960).

Carrol Lewis, *Jabberwocky* in *Through the Looking Glass* (1871).

Coleridge Samuel Taylor, *Dejection, An Ode* (1802).

Fitzgerald Nicholas (1985) *Brian Jones, The Inside Story of the Original Rolling Stones,*

G.P. Putnam's Sons, Toronto (1985).

Goethe von Johan Wolfgang, (1808-1832) *Faust.*

Jackson Laura, *Brian Jones, The untold life and mysterious death of a rock legend*, Piatkus, London (2009).

Jonson Ben, poem *Short Measures.*

Kafka Franz *Brief and Den Vater,* CreateSpace Independent Publishing Platform (2016), originally published in 1952, after being written in 1919 Korner Alexis online resources Lancet, 1976.

Mayall John, *Blues from Laurel Canyon, My Life as a Bluesman,* Omnibus Press (2019).

Melody Maker magazine, 23 April 1966.

Mirror magazine, February 1966.

Osler, William, *The Principles and Practice of Medicine.* D. Appleton & Company, New York 1912, first published in 1892.

Proust Marcel, *letters.*

Rawlings Terry, *Brian Jones, Who Killed Christopher Robin?* e-book published by RockBookShop (2013).

Rolling Stone magazine online, 17 June 2017.

Rollings Stones Chronicles online.

Salter, Henry, *On Asthma: Its Pathology and Treatment.* Churchill & Sons, London (1860).

Stach Reiner, *Kafka: The Decisive Years,* Princeton University Press (2013).

Trynka Paul, *Brian Jones, The Making of the Rolling Stones*, Plume, Penguin Random House, London (2014).

Wilder Thornton (1927) *The Bridge of San Luis Rey,* Albert & Charles Boni, NY (1927).

Wyman Bill with Ray Coleman, *Stone Alone, The Story of a Rock'n'Roll Band,* Da Capo Press, New York (1997).

Basic Further Eye-Openers

Bradshaw, John, (1988), *The Family.*

Brown Nina W, *Children of the Self-Absorbed* (2008).

Forward, Susan, PhD, *Emotional Blackmail* (2001).

Forward, Susan, PhD, *Toxic Parents* (2008).

Peurifoy Reneau Z, *Anxiety, Phobias and Panic* (2005).

References

[1] Terry Rawlings, *Brian Jones-who killed Christopher Robin?* p. 20.

[2] Bill Wyman, *Stone Alone* p. 356.

[3] Wyman, Ibid p. 103.

[4] Rawlings, Ibid p. 57.

[5] *Daily Mail,* article by Christopher Stevens and Sam Creighton, 23 May 2015.

[6] Field T, Vega-Lahr N, Scafidi F, Goldstein S., *Effects of maternal unavailability on mother-infant interactions.* Infant Behavior and Development (1986).

[7] Stach, Reiner, (2005) *Kafka the Decisive Years*, pp. 44, 207.

[8] Brod, Max, (1960) *Franz Kafka, A Biography.*

[9] Laura Jackson, *Brian Jones, The untold life and mysterious death of a rock legend,* p. 22.

[10] Adams F, *The Genuine Works of Hippocrates.* London, The Sydenham Society, 1849.

[11] Salter, Henry Hyde *On Asthma: Its Pathology and Treatment.* London, John Churchill and Sons, 1860.

[12] Osler, William, *The Principles and Practice of Medicine.* New York, D. Appleton and Company, 1892.

[13] Paul Trynka, *Brian Jones, the Making of the Rolling Stones*, p.18.
[14] Jackson, Ibid p. 10.
[15] Danny Garcia's film *The Life and Death of Brian Jones*.
[16] Nicholas Fitzgerald, *Brian Jones: The Inside Story of The Original Rolling Stone*, p. 234.
[17] Wyman, Ibid p. 100.
[18] Wyman, Ibid p. 199.
[19] *Mirror* magazine, February 1966.
[20] *Melody Maker* magazine, 23 April 1966.
[21] *Rolling Stone* magazine online, 17 June 2017.
[22] Fitzgerald, Ibid p. 235.
[23] Newspaper article by Don Short in *The Mirror* in 1969.
[24] Copy of a newspaper clipping without a source or date.
[25] Jackson, Ibid p. 5.
[26] *Rolling Stones Chronicles 1968* online, http://www.timeisonourside .com/chron1968.html.
[27] Newspaper clipping.
[28] Newspaper clipping.
[29] Paul Trynka, *Brian Jones, The Making Of The Rolling Stones,* p.310.
[30] John Mayall, *Blues from Laurel Canyon*, Omnibus Press, p. 177.
[31] Fitzgerald, Ibid p.232.
[32] Fitzgerald, Ibid p. 234.
[33] Article in German teen magazine *BRAVO* on 16 June 1969.
[34] Danny Garcia's film *The Life and Death of Brian Jones*.
[35] *British medical Journal.* 1976, 1, 404; *Lancet*, 1976, 1, 374.
[36] Wyman, Ibid pp. 352–353.

[37] https://www.nme.com/news/music/fresh-evidence-rolling-stones-brian-jones-murder-new-netflix-documentary-2533208. Brian Jones- Crimewatch 1994 documentary.
[38] Fitzgerald, Ibid pp. 239–240.
[39] Wyman, Ibid p. 530.
[40] Wyman, Ibid p. 535.
[41] Fitzgerald, Ibid p. 241.
[42] Fitzgerald, Ibid p. 250.
[43] Fitzgerald, Ibid p. 241.
[44] Rawlings, Ibid p. 147.